DAVE ARMSTRONG

100 Biblical Arguments
Against *Sola Scriptura*

CATHOLIC
ANSWERS
PRESS

SAN DIEGO
2012

100 Biblical Arguments Against *Sola Scriptura*
© 2012 by Dave Armstrong

Unless otherwise noted, biblical citations are taken from the Revised Standard Version of the Bible
(© 1971 by Division of Christian Education of the National Council of the Churches of Christ in the United States of America).

Published by Catholic Answers, Inc.
2020 Gillespie Way
El Cajon, California 92020
1-888-291-8000 orders
619-387-0042 fax
catholic.com

Cover design by Devin Schadt
Interior design by Russell Design
Printed in the United States of America
ISBN 978-1-933919-59-1

For related reading on the author's blog, see:
The Bible, Church, Tradition, and Canon
http://socrates58.blogspot.com/2006/11/bible-church-tradition-canon-index.html
The Church
http://socrates58.blogspot.com/2006/11/church-index-page.html
The Papacy
http://socrates58.blogspot.com/2006/11/papacy-index-page.html

To my wife Judy and children Paul,
Michael, Matthew, and Angelina:
Thank you for the gift of your love and
understanding, and for being who you are.
I've been blessed beyond all imagining.

Contents

Introduction

Catholicism and Protestantism differ fundamentally with regard to authority—the "rule of faith," the basis or standard Christians use to determine true (and false) doctrine and practice. Protestantism tends to see a divide between the "pure Word of God" in the Bible and what the Catholic Church calls Sacred Tradition—something Protestantism considers to be corrupted by "traditions of men" (Matt. 15:3-6; Mark 7:8-13). For Protestants, Scripture alone is the source and rule of the Christian faith. It is the only infallible authority, sufficient in and of itself for a full exposition of Christianity and for the attainment of salvation. This is what *sola scriptura* means. In Catholicism, by contrast, Scripture *and* Tradition—revealed Christian truths passed on outside of Scripture—are two fonts of the one spring of divine revelation. Without one or the other, revelation is incomplete.

Scripture frequently refers to the notion of *tradition[s]*: a body of knowledge or doctrine that existed prior to and is larger than Scripture itself. For example:

> Acts 17:11, 13: Now these Jews were more noble than those in Thessaloni'ca, for they received the word with all eagerness, examining the scriptures daily to see if these things were so. . . . But when the Jews of Thessaloni'ca learned that the word of God was proclaimed by Paul at Beroe'a also, they came there too, stirring up and inciting the crowds.

The "word" or "word of God" in this context is clearly not Scripture, because Scripture is compared with it; it is, rather, apostolic preaching, which is synonymous with sacred Tradition. All true Tradition, like the preaching that is examined in the above passage, is harmonious with Scripture. This is the biblical and Catholic teaching.

Other terms besides "word of God" are used in the Bible to

refer to apostolic Tradition, such as "the faith" (Eph. 4:13; Col. 1:23; 1 Tim. 4:1; Jude 3), "the truth" (Rom. 2:8; Gal. 5:7; 1 Tim. 2:4), "the commandment" (Mark 7:8; 2 Pet. 2:21; 1 John 2:7–8), "the doctrine" (Rom. 16:17; Titus 2:10; 2 John 1:9), and "the message" (1 Cor. 2:4; 2 Cor. 5:19; 2 Tim. 4:15). The biblical data on this score are overwhelming. A concise Catholic definition of sacred Tradition is found in the decrees of the First Vatican Council (1870), in the *Dogmatic Constitution on the Catholic Faith*:

> This supernatural revelation, according to the universal belief of the Church, declared by the sacred Synod of Trent, is contained in the written books and unwritten traditions which, received by the Apostles from the mouth of Christ himself, or from the Apostles themselves, by the dictation of the Holy Spirit, transmitted, as it were, from hand to hand, have come down even to us.[1]

There are many complexities and nuances involved in this discussion of Christian authority that will become apparent as we delve into it. Catholics and Protestants have misunderstood each other for centuries. Yet, although there are deeply held differences, there is also more common ground than one might suspect.

Before going any further, I should like to verify the preceding definitions of *sola scriptura* by citing three of its contemporary Protestant defenders. Norman Geisler, a prominent Evangelical Protestant apologist who has published many books, defines it as follows:

> By *sola scriptura* orthodox Protestants mean that Scripture alone is the primary and absolute source of authority, the final court of appeal, for all doctrine and practice (faith and morals). It is important to repeat that Catholics often misunderstand the Protestant principle of *sola scriptura* to exclude any truth outside the Bible. This, of course, is untrue. . . . What Protestants mean by *sola scriptura* is that the Bible alone is the

infallible written authority for faith and morals. . . . Scripture is the sufficient and final written authority of God. As to sufficiency, the Bible—nothing more, nothing less, and nothing else—is all that is necessary for faith and practice . . . the Bible is clear (perspicuous). The perspicuity of Scripture does not mean that everything in the Bible is perfectly clear, but rather the essential teachings are. Popularly put, in the Bible the main things are the plain things and the plain things are the main things. This is not to say that Protestants obtain no help from the Fathers and early councils . . . this is not to say that there is no usefulness to Christian tradition, but only that it is of secondary importance.[2]

Reformed Protestant writer Keith A. Mathison concurs, while emphasizing the role of the Church a little more strongly:

Scripture alone is inspired and inherently infallible. Scripture alone is the supreme normative standard. But Scripture does not exist in a vacuum. It was and is given to the Church within the doctrinal context of the apostolic gospel. Scripture alone is the only final standard, but it is a final standard that must be utilized, interpreted, and preached by the Church within its Christian context.

It is important to notice that *sola scriptura*, properly understood, is not a claim that Scripture is the only authority altogether. . . . There are other real authorities which are subordinate and derivative in nature. Scripture, however, is the only inspired and inherently infallible norm, and therefore Scripture is the only final authoritative norm.[3]

He adds, "It must be emphasized that the fallibility of the Church does not render her authority invalid."[4]

Reformed Baptist James R. White, despite belonging to the extreme anti-Catholic fundamentalist wing of Protestantism, nevertheless agrees with Geisler and Mathison in this respect, as we see in his series of expositions detailing first what *sola scriptura* is not:

1. *First and foremost, sola scriptura is not a claim that the Bible contains all knowledge.*
2. *Sola scriptura is not a claim that the Bible is an exhaustive catalog of all* religious *knowledge.* . . . It is obvious that the Bible does not need to be exhaustive to be sufficient as our source of divine truth.
3. *Sola scriptura is not a denial of the authority of the Church to teach God's truth* . . . The Church, as the body of Christ, presents and upholds the truth, but she remains subservient to it. . . . There is no warrant for the "Lone Ranger Christian Syndrome" so popular in Protestant circles these days.
4. *Sola scriptura is not a denial that the Word of God has, at times, been spoken.* Rather, it refers to the Scriptures as serving the Church as God's final and full revelation. . . . It is vitally important that the reader recognize that the Protestant position insists that all God intends for us to have that is infallible, binding, and authoritative today, He has already provided in the certain, clear, understandable, and reliable Scriptures.
5. *Sola scriptura does not entail the rejection of every kind or form of "tradition."* There are some traditions that are God-honoring and useful in the Church. *Sola scriptura* simply means that any tradition, no matter how ancient or venerable it might seem to us, must be tested by a higher authority, and that authority is the Bible.
6. *Sola scriptura is not a denial of the role of the Holy Spirit in guiding and enlightening the Church.*

White then proceeds to show what *sola scriptura* is:

1. *The doctrine of sola scriptura, simply stated, is that the Scriptures alone are sufficient to function as the* regulafidei, *the infallible rule of faith for the Church.*
2. *All that one* must *believe to be a Christian is found in Scripture, and in no other source.*

3. *That which is not found in Scripture—either directly or by necessary implication—is not binding upon the Christian.*
4. *Scripture reveals those things necessary for salvation.*
5. *All traditions are subject to the higher authority of Scripture.*[5]

In this book, I will be presupposing the above definitions of *sola scriptura:* good and clear definitions from three of its ablest defenders. Let the reader take note! For it is the almost-invariable practice of Protestants to accuse Catholics of not understanding what *sola scriptura* is in the first place. I'm sure there are many Catholics who don't understand. But I *do* understand what *sola scriptura* is. I used to adhere to it myself, precisely in these terms, and I defended it, as a Protestant apologist and evangelist, for nine years. I know what it is, and I reject it as a falsehood.

Let me conclude with a word on my premises and methodology. The discussion of Christian authority is rife with miscomprehensions on both sides. People are used to reading unsophisticated and inadequate treatments of *sola scriptura* from both proponents and opponents.

It is not enough, therefore, merely to cite biblical evidences of Tradition or an authoritative Church. These things are not, by their mere mention, sufficient to refute *sola scriptura* (as our three Protestant proponents cited above point out). The Catholic needs to go further than that and establish, based on unassailable biblical evidence, examples of Tradition or of Church proclamations that were *binding* and *obligatory* upon all who heard and received them. Whether these were *infallible* is a more complex question, but a binding decree is already either expressly contrary to *sola scriptura*, or, at the very least, casts considerable doubt on the formal principle.

Thus, one of my favorite counter-arguments is to point out that the Apostle Paul and his companions Silas and Timothy made their way "through the cities" and "delivered to them for observance the decisions which had been reached by the apostles and elders who were at Jerusalem" (Acts 16:4). This council at Jerusalem was described in the previous chapter as having reached its decisions by the direct aid or guidance of the Holy Spirit (15:28).

When we put all of that together we see an infallible council, presided over by bishops (Peter: Acts 15:7-11; and James: 15:13-21), and proclaimed by an apostle (Paul). It was a development of Tradition and Mosaic Law (about circumcision and what was proper to eat) and a binding exercise of Church authority at the highest levels; even seemingly infallible. All of this is strong counter-indication of *sola scriptura*, which proclaims that no Church or council can bind the conscience of a Christian believer, or can claim to be infallible. For the Protestant, only Scripture can do that. Yet here the same Scripture seems to refute that very proposition.

This is how one goes about refuting *sola scriptura:* by demonstrating how biblical teaching makes the Protestant rule of faith collapse into self-contradictions and incoherence. It's a death by a thousand qualifications (and worse).

PART ONE

The Binding Authority
of the Tradition

I.
Biblical and Apostolic Tradition Contrasted with the False and Corrupt Traditions of Men

1. The Bible contains much information on Sacred Tradition

Scripture is unique, but it refers to an authoritative apostolic tradition apart from itself:

> 1 Corinthians 11:2: I commend you because you remember me in everything and maintain the traditions even as I have delivered them to you.

> 2 Thessalonians 2:15: So then, brethren, stand firm and hold to the traditions which you were taught by us, either by word of mouth or by letter.

> 2 Thessalonians 3:6: Now we command you, brethren, in the name of our Lord Jesus Christ, that you keep away from any brother who is living in idleness and not in accord with the tradition that you received from us.

> 2 Peter 2:21: For it would have been better for them never to have known the way of righteousness than after knowing it to turn back from the holy commandment delivered to them.

When Paul spoke of receiving and delivering such traditions, he gave no indication that they were fallible or that he questioned any of them because they came through oral transmission rather than the written word. Thus, he appears to take for granted that which many Protestants have the hardest time grasping and accepting.

The related Greek words *paradidomi* and *paralambano* are usually rendered, respectively, as (traditions) "delivered" (Luke 1:1-2; Rom. 6:17; 1 Cor. 11:2, 23; 15:3; 2 Pet. 2:21; Jude 3) and "received" (1 Cor. 11:23; 15:1-3; Gal. 1:9, 12; 1 Thess. 2:13).

2. In the Bible, good (apostolic) Tradition is contrasted with bad traditions of men

The bottom (biblical) line is not "tradition versus no tradition," but rather, "true, apostolic tradition versus false traditions of men." The Bible often expressly distinguishes between the two (false tradition is italicized in the following passages; true tradition bolded):

> Matthew 15:3: He answered them, "And why do you *transgress* **the commandment of God** for the sake of *your tradition?*"

> Matthew 15:6: So, for the sake of *your tradition*, you have *made void* **the word of God**.

> Matthew 15:9: "*In vain* do they worship me, teaching as **doctrines** *the precepts of men.*"

> Matthew 16:23: But he turned and said to Peter, "Get behind me, Satan! You are a hindrance to me; for you are *not* **on the side of God**, *but of men*" (cf. Mark 8:33).

> Mark 7:8-9, 13: "You *leave* the **commandment of God**, and hold fast *the tradition of men.*" And he said to them, "You have a fine way of *rejecting* the **commandment of God**, in order to keep *your tradition!* . . . thus *making void* **the word of God** through *your tradition* which you hand on."

> 1 Corinthians 2:13: And we impart this in **words** *not taught by human wisdom* **but taught by the Spirit**, interpreting **spiritual truths** to those who possess the Spirit.

> Galatians 1:9-12: As we have said before, so now I say again,

If anyone is preaching to you *a gospel contrary to* **that which you received**, let him be accursed. Am I now seeking the *favor of men*, or **of God**? Or am I trying to *please men*? If I were still *pleasing men*, I should not be a **servant of Christ**. For I would have you know, brethren, that **the gospel which was preached by me** is not *man's gospel*. For I **did not** *receive it from man*, nor was I taught it, but **it came through a revelation of Jesus Christ**.

Colossians 2:8: See to it that no one makes a prey of you by *philosophy and empty deceit, according to human tradition*, according to the *elemental spirits of the universe*, and not **according to Christ**.

1 Thessalonians 2:13: And we also thank God constantly for this, that when you received **the word of God which you heard from us**, you accepted it not as *the word of men* but as what it really is, **the word of God**, which is at work in you believers.

1 Timothy 4:1, 6-7: Now the Spirit expressly says that in later times some will *depart from the faith* by giving heed to *deceitful spirits and doctrines of demons* . . . If you put **these instructions** before the brethren, you will be a good minister of Christ Jesus, nourished on **the words of the faith and of the good doctrine** which you have followed. Have nothing to do with *godless and silly myths*. Train yourself in **godliness**.

3. Peter exercises apostolic authority in Acts 2

In his sermon in the upper room (Acts 2) and in other recorded sermons, St. Peter gives an authoritative New Covenant interpretation of salvation history, interpreting the Old Testament messianically and "Christianly." It was binding and equally authoritative and inspired before it became "inscripturated" because it was from an apostle. Throughout the book of

Acts we see Peter and Paul exercising apostolic authority and preaching—not merely handing out Bibles or mouthing (Old Testament) Scripture.

4. The Bible explicitly teaches about a true and unchangeable apostolic Tradition

Tradition, like the Bible or the Word of God, is presented as immutable in Scripture: delivered "once for all" to the saints. This preached gospel stood forever as truth before it was ever encapsulated in the Bible.

> Acts 2:42: And they devoted themselves to the apostles' teaching and fellowship, to the breaking of bread and the prayers.

> Jude 3: I found it necessary to write appealing to you to contend for the faith which was once for all delivered to the saints.

5. Tradition is an inevitable reality for all Christians

It should be noted that all Christian groups have *some* traditions, whether or not they acknowledge it. (*Sola scriptura* is one of them.) If a Calvinist, for example, were to start interpreting certain Scripture passages about falling away from grace and from the faith as suggesting something other than perseverance of the saints or eternal security, he would be suspect in the eyes of his Calvinist comrades. He would not be allowed to interpret the Bible in such a way within his circle of fellow Calvinist believers—*sola scriptura* or no, perspicuity of Scripture or no, supremacy of conscience and private judgment or no. Thus, there is a limit to how far a Calvinist can go in interpreting Scripture, and that limit is set by Calvinist tradition.

If a Lutheran (Missouri Synod) pastor started asserting that the Eucharist and baptism were purely symbolic, he would be in big trouble, since confessional, orthodox Lutheranism holds

to the Real Presence—consubstantiation —and baptismal regeneration. If a Baptist pastor or theologian adopted a belief
in infant baptism, he would be told that he doesn't see the
clear evidence of Scripture for an adult, believer's baptism, and
would probably soon be out of a job— and so on.

The Catholic Church, too, has parameters of orthodoxy beyond which a Catholic may not go. There may be relatively *more*
of these, but the restrictions are not different *in kind* from Protestant restrictions on dogma, hermeneutics, and exegesis. Thus, all
Christian groups, not just the Catholic Church, employ tradition
to shape and curb the way their followers interpret Scripture.

6. "Not in the Bible" doesn't mean "anti-biblical"

That a tradition is extra-biblical does not mean that it is non-
biblical or unbiblical or contrary to the Bible. It simply means
that it is not explicitly contained within the letter of the Bible,
though it might well be in *harmony* with it. But a certain kind
of Protestant hears "extra-biblical" and immediately equates
that with "fallible traditions of men that are obviously contrary
to Scripture." And yet it is *this* idea that is contrary to Scripture, not the notion of tradition per se.

It is absurd to presume that because a particular oral or
Church tradition is not explicitly taught in the Bible it is false,
and that the apostles intended for all Christian teaching after
their deaths to be located in the written word of the Bible
alone. It is the fallacy of "argument from silence"—asserting a
conclusion based on lack of evidence to the contrary. It is also
self-defeating, for if *sola scriptura* were true, it would *have to be*
explicitly spelled out in Scripture itself. Yet it is not.

7. Covenants and Sacred Tradition are perpetually binding

The ancient Jews had the Mosaic Law and the Davidic Covenant: a
clear, identifiable tradition that didn't change when corruption oc-

curred, as it did cyclically. They kept discovering the Law and their God again and again, and (in their better moments) cooperated with God's revival of their hearts and behavior. Corruption didn't wipe out the Law anymore than David's sin wiped out the Davidic Covenant, or Paul's or Moses' or Peter's sin made them incapable of writing inspired Scripture and being leaders of their people.

8. Apostolic Tradition is in harmony with Scripture

The apostolic deposit—the body of theological and moral doctrine received from Jesus, passed on to the apostles, and passed down by them—is not "secondary" material. It expands upon what we know from Scripture, and though it is not inspired like the Bible, its truths are every bit as revealed and infallible.

Truth doesn't *have* to be in the Bible to be authoritative (see biblical references to teachings and acts not recorded: Matt. 13:3; Mark 4:2, 33; 6:34; Luke 11:53; 24:15-16, 25-27; John 16:12; 20:30; 21:25; Acts 1:2-3). It has to be apostolic and to have always been held implicitly or explicitly by the Church universal:

> Jude 3: I found it necessary to write appealing to you to contend for the faith which was once for all delivered to the saints.

What is apostolic will always be harmonious with biblical teachings, since the truths Jesus taught the apostles and the truths recorded in Scripture proceed from the same body of God's revelation.

9. Authoritative interpretation of the Law was required in ancient Israel

Moses certainly gave definitive interpretation of doctrine, as did the priesthood in Israel. What they read from "the book" did not interpret itself.

> Nehemiah 8:7-8: Also Jesh'ua, Bani, Sherebi'ah, Jamin, Akkub,

Shab'bethai, Hodi'ah, Ma-asei'ah, Keli'ta, Azari'ah, Jo'zabad, Hanan, Pelai'ah, the Levites, helped the people to understand the law, while the people remained in their places. And they read from the book, from the law of God, clearly; and they gave the sense, so that the people understood the reading.

10. In Scripture, the infallible nature of Pauline tradition is taken for granted

Paul assumed that his passed-down tradition was binding and therefore infallible. Were Paul not assuming that, he would have been commanding his followers to adhere to a mistaken doctrine.

2 Thessalonians 3:14: If any one refuses to obey what we say in this letter, note that man, and have nothing to do with him, that he may be ashamed.

Romans 16:17: Take note of those who create dissensions and difficulties, in opposition to the doctrine which you have been taught; avoid them.

11. "Commandment" and "command" are synonyms for Tradition

In the Bible these words are used in a generic sense to mean God's truth—binding traditions that originate outside of Scripture.

Romans 7:8-13: But sin, finding opportunity in the commandment, wrought in me all kinds of covetousness. Apart from the law sin lies dead. I was once alive apart from the law, but when the commandment came, sin revived and I died; the very commandment which promised life proved to be death to me. For sin, finding opportunity in the commandment, deceived me and by it killed me. So the law is holy, and the commandment is holy and just and good. Did that which is good, then, bring death to me? By no means!

It was sin, working death in me through what is good, in order that sin might be shown to be sin, and through the commandment might become sinful beyond measure.

Romans 16:25-27: Now to him who is able to strengthen you according to my gospel and the preaching of Jesus Christ, according to the revelation of the mystery which was kept secret for long ages but is now disclosed and through the prophetic writings is made known to all nations, according to the command of the eternal God, to bring about the obedience of faith— to the only wise God be glory for evermore through Jesus Christ!

2 Peter 3:2: That you should remember the predictions of the holy prophets and the commandment of the Lord and Savior through your apostles.

1 John 2:7: Beloved, I am writing you no new commandment, but an old commandment which you had from the beginning; the old commandment is the word which you have heard.

12. Pauline tradition was shared with and by other apostles

2 Thessalonians was conveyed or partially written by Silvanus and Timothy also, according to 2 Thessalonians 1:1. Paul (as the presumed primary author) often uses the plural "we" or "us" (see, e.g., 1:3-4, 11; 2:1, 13). Thus, in 2 Thessalonians 2:15, when he enjoins readers to hold fast to "traditions which you were taught, whether by word of mouth or by letter from us," Paul is asserting that not only is his own instruction authoritative, but also that of Silvanus and Timothy. This undercuts the contextual argument that Paul was the "pastor of the Thessalonians." Paul later reiterates this plurality:

2 Thessalonians 3:6-7: Now we command you, brethren, in the name of our Lord Jesus Christ, that you keep away from every brother who is living in idleness and not in accord with the tradition that you received from us. For you yourselves know how you ought to imitate us; we were not idle when we were with you.

We see, then, that this tradition was larger than simply Paul's own teaching, which later (in the oft-expressed Protestant view) would be recorded in the Bible and there alone. Catholics agree that Scripture contains this deposit, but not all of it *explicitly* or not *every jot and tittle* of apostolic tradition.

II.
Oral and Deuterocanonical Tradition

13. The New Testament cites traditions that are not spelled out in the Old Testament

Many Protestants simply assume without argument that anything that is authoritative must be in the Bible. Yet, in the New Testament we read authoritative citations of unwritten traditions.

> Matthew 2:23: And he went and dwelt in a city called Nazareth, that what was spoken by the prophets might be fulfilled, "He shall be called a Nazarene."

This reference cannot be found in the Old Testament, yet it was nevertheless passed down "by the prophets."

> Matthew 23:1-3: ("Moses' seat"; already seen above.)

> 1 Corinthians 10:4: And all drank the same supernatural drink. For they drank from the supernatural Rock which followed them, and the Rock was Christ.

The Old Testament says nothing about any miraculous movement of the rock that Moses struck to produce water (Exod. 17:1-7; Num. 20:2-13). But rabbinic tradition does.[6]

> 2 Timothy 3:8: As Jannes and Jambres opposed Moses, so these men also oppose the truth, men of corrupt mind and counterfeit faith.

These two men cannot be found in the related Old Testament passage (Exod. 7:8 ff.) or anywhere else in the Old Testament.

> 1 Peter 3:18-20: For Christ also died for sins once for all, the

righteous for the unrighteous, that he might bring us to God, being put to death in the flesh but made alive in the spirit; in which he went and preached to the spirits in prison, who formerly did not obey, when God's patience waited in the days of Noah, during the building of the ark, in which a few, that is, eight persons, were saved through water.

Peter, in describing Christ's journey to Sheol/Hades, draws directly from the Jewish apocalyptic book 1 Enoch (12-16).

Jude 9: But when the archangel Michael, contending with the devil, disputed about the body of Moses, he did not presume to pronounce a reviling judgment upon him, but said, "The Lord rebuke you."

Jude 14-15: It was of these also that Enoch in the seventh generation from Adam prophesied, saying, "Behold, the Lord came with his holy myriads, to execute judgment on all, and to convict all the ungodly of all their deeds of ungodliness which they have committed in such an ungodly way, and of all the harsh things which ungodly sinners have spoken against him."

Here Jude directly cites 1 Enoch 1:9, and even asserts that Enoch prophesied.

Since Jesus and the apostles acknowledge authoritative Jewish oral and extra-biblical tradition (even in so doing raising some of it to the level of written revelation), we are hardly at liberty to assert that it is altogether illegitimate. If some extra-biblical traditions and notions (that is, those outside of the Old Testament, which was the only Scripture that existed in Jesus' time) can be held as true and authoritative, then it stands to reason that others can be, too.

14. The informal discussions of Jesus and the apostles are dynamically and organically related to Tradition and Scripture

In a single night of discussion, Jesus—or Paul, or other apostles passing along what they learned from our Lord—could easily have spoken more words than we have in the entire New Testament. It is implausible to think none of that had any effect on the subsequent teaching of these same apostles and disciples. One can remember encounters with extraordinary people for a lifetime—at least the main ideas, if not all particulars. Here are several examples of life-changing encounters with the apostle Paul, as a result of his vigorously sharing the gospel and apostolic Tradition with his hearers, at the greatest length (not merely citing Bible verses or passing out Old Testaments):

> Acts 17:1-4: Now when they had passed through Amphip'olis and Apollo'nia, they came to Thessaloni'ca, where there was a synagogue of the Jews. And Paul went in, as was his custom, and for three weeks he argued with them from the scriptures, explaining and proving that it was necessary for the Christ to suffer and to rise from the dead, and saying, "This Jesus, whom I proclaim to you, is the Christ." And some of them were persuaded, and joined Paul and Silas; as did a great many of the devout Greeks and not a few of the leading women.

> Acts 17:17: So he argued in the synagogue with the Jews and the devout persons, and in the market place every day with those who chanced to be there (cf. 18:4, 19).

> Acts 19:8-10: And he entered the synagogue and for three months spoke boldly, arguing and pleading about the kingdom of God; but when some were stubborn and disbelieved, speaking evil of the Way before the congregation, he withdrew from them, taking the disciples with him, and argued daily in the hall of Tyran'nus. This continued for two years, so that all the residents of Asia heard the word of the Lord, both Jews and Greeks.

15. The Bible never says that oral tradition would cease

Protestants will often acknowledge, when pressed, that authoritative oral teachings existed before Scripture was compiled, but then are quick to add that the written Bible obviated the need for them (and indeed, *sola scriptura* holds this by definition), so they ceased. Yet, the Bible says no such thing. It can't be found anywhere. Thus, the Protestant notion of "no tradition after Scripture" is itself a false "tradition of men."

16. The New Testament frequently cites Deuterocanonical books

Since Protestants consider the deuterocanonical books of the Old Testament (which they term the "Apocrypha") to be non-inspired and thus not part of the Bible, to cite them is, from their perspective, to cite an extra-biblical tradition. Yet, from Jesus and the New Testament writer we find a multitude of allusions to and citations of the deuterocanonical books. Here is a selection of examples from just the Gospel of Matthew:

Matthew 4:4 (cites Wisdom 16:26)
Matthew 4:15 (1 Maccabees 5:15)
Matthew 5:18 (Baruch 4:1)
Matthew 5:28 (Sirach 9:8)
Matthew 5:4 (Sirach 48:24)
Matthew 6:7 (Sirach 7:14)
Matthew 6:9 (Sirach 23:1, 4)
Matthew 6:10 (1 Maccabees 3:60)
Matthew 6:12 (Sirach 28:2)
Matthew 6:13 (Sirach 33:1)
Matthew 6:20 (Sirach 29:10-12)
Matthew 7:12 (Tobit 4:15; Sirach 31:15)
Matthew 7:16 (Sirach 27:6)
Matthew 8:11 (Baruch 4:37)
Matthew 9:36 (Judith 11:19)

Matthew 10:16 (Sirach 13:17)
Matthew 11:14 (Sirach 48:1–10)
Matthew 11:29 (Sirach 6:23–31; 51:26–27)
Matthew 12:4 (2 Maccabees 10:3)
Matthew 13:44 (Sirach 20:30–31)
Matthew 16:18 (Wisdom 16:13)
Matthew 16:27 (Sirach 35:18–19)
Matthew 17:11 (Sirach 48:10)
Matthew 18:10 (Tobit 12:15)
Matthew 23:38 (Tobit 14:4)
Matthew 27:24 (Susanna 1:46; Daniel 13:46 in Catholic bibles)
Matthew 27:43 (Wisdom 2:12–22)

17. Competing schools in Judaism are analogous to denominations in Protestantism

Some Protestants will argue that because there were two
schools of interpretation in later pharisaical and early rabbinic
Judaism (schools of Hillel and Shammai), or because there were
diverse communities of Judaism beyond Pharisaism, such as the
Sadducees and the Essenes, that the very notion of authoritative oral tradition must be discarded. For example, Reformed
Baptist and prominent anti-Catholic apologist James White
contends, in an Internet article:

> The tractate indicates that the Torah was passed down to
> such individuals as Shammai and Hillel, yet, as students of
> NT backgrounds know, these two set up opposing schools
> with different understandings of tradition (should sound fa-
> miliar!). Who was, in fact, the true recipient of this alleged
> oral tradition, then?[7]

Why, then, are the Protestants (such as White) who make
such a critique not similarly troubled by the far *more* diverse,
often contradictory state of affairs in Protestantism as a result of

sola scriptura? They believe that the Bible is the sole rule of faith and that its teachings are clear, yet so many are apparently unable to interpret those teachings correctly. If the evidence for oral tradition in Judaism is nullified because there were competing schools of interpretation, then all the more should the contradictory and competing interpretive traditions in Protestantism nullify the principle of *sola scriptura*.

The bottom line is not that there may be differences and even schools within an overall theology, but rather, the necessity for an *authoritative interpretation*. In Catholicism, that is provided by the Church. Protestantism cannot resolve its internal differences because, by rejecting the notion of an infallible Church, it has ruled out any human agencies that could resolve them definitively. All parties appeal to the Bible, but within the denominational system there is no way to declare authoritatively who is right and wrong. Without apostolic succession and the passing-down of apostolic tradition through ordained bishops, Protestants are reduced to "the magisterium of academics," or to competing votes of the leaders of relatively small denominational bodies. To some extent this was also true of the Jews at the time of the advent of Christianity, but it is *not* true of Catholicism.

18. Divine prophetic truth is always present alongside written Scripture

No one would be foolish enough to claim that *every* sermon, plea, or prophetic warning of Jeremiah or any of the other prophets was recorded in writing and preserved in the Bible. In one long night alone, if Jeremiah had kept talking, we'd have more words than are contained in the entire book named for him. These words were, in many instances, the "word of the Lord," even though not later recorded for posterity in Scripture.

Likewise, not all the words of the Lord were recorded; for

example, Jesus' words explaining the messianic prophecies about himself, spoken to the two disciples on the road to Emmaus, were not recorded, but they were true, and inspired, since they came from Jesus himself (see Luke 24:26-27). Those who heard both Jeremiah and Jesus were bound to obey their words—before they were written down and regardless of whether they were *ever* written down.

19. Inscripturation is not the final determinant of binding truthfulness

When Paul was preaching to the Corinthians, Galatians, Thessalonians, et al, he preached authoritatively, as an apostle. Not everything he said was later included in the Bible; therefore, it was not all *inspired* (he was no walking Bible-machine any more than Jesus was). But he was an *authority*, and acted consciously upon this authority.

Some Protestants who hold to extreme variants of *sola scriptura*, on the other hand, would have us believe that his authority, in the final analysis, depends upon the Christian being able to read an epistle of Paul's, knowing that it was part of the New Testament, and doing so without the aid of an authoritative Church that could declare what was Scripture and make the canon binding on all Christians.

This is directly implied in some Protestant arguments contending that *everything* Paul taught, including every tradition to which he alludes, was later inscripturated. Thus, anything *not* recorded in Scripture could not have been taught or passed down by Paul, so the flip side of the same proposition would hold—a contention that is absurd on its face.

Sixteenth-century Anglican apologist William Whitaker asserts this in his elaborate defense of *sola scriptura* (highly touted by proponents today, especially anti-Catholic ones), entitled *A Disputation on Holy Scripture*:[8]

I confess that Christ said many things about the kingdom, but of the popish traditions not a word. . . . From Matt, xxviii., Mark xvi., John xx. and xxi., Luke xxiv., and Acts i., we may gather the nature of his discourses. He expounded to them the scriptures; he gave them authority to cast out devils, to retain and remit sins; he attested his resurrection to them; he bade them preach the gospel to all nations, and said other things of the same kind, which we can read in scripture, so that we have no need of such conjectures as the papists rely upon in this question (p. 548).

The things which Paul delivered orally were not different from, but absolutely the same with, those which were written (p. 552).

The Jesuit answers, in the second place, that, even though it were conceded that all is written in other books, yet this would be no objection to believing in traditions also. For (says he) the apostle does not say, I promise that I or the other apostles will commit all the rest to writing, but, "hold the traditions." I answer; Although Paul had never written or made such a promise, does it follow that all the rest were not written by other apostles? (p. 554).

The third place cited by the Jesuit in this fourth testimony is contained in 2 Tim. ii. 2, where Paul thus addresses Timothy: "Those things which thou hast heard of me before many witnesses, the same commit thou to faithful men, who shall be able to instruct others also." . . . The apostle in these words commends sound doctrine to Timothy, and that no other than what is contained in the scriptures (p. 557).

This assumption—that no legitimate apostolic traditions could possibly have been passed down that are not also explicitly laid out in Scripture—is not found anywhere in Scripture itself. Since it is based on no solid evidence, whether biblical or historiographical, and, as seen, is contradicted by many biblical indications, we can safely dismiss it— as most Protestants do.

20. Oral tradition is wider in scope than Scripture

It is certainly not clear (either from the Bible alone or from logic) that Paul's oral teaching (e.g., 1 Cor. 11:2, 23; 15:1-3; Gal. 1:9, 12; 1 Thess. 2:13; 2 Thess. 3:6; 2 Tim. 1:13-14; 2:2) must be the same as his written teaching, or that it couldn't contain information not found in his letters. We can reasonably deduce from later patristic testimony and biblical indications that Paul's oral teaching would be harmonious with his teaching now preserved in the Bible; but it also would almost certainly have contained some things not found in Scripture.

Virtually all of what we know about Paul's teaching is contained in the Bible; yet we can show that he taught a great deal more that could not possibly all be recorded in Holy Writ. Number fourteen above, for example, shows how he argued and reasoned in the synagogues and other public places. The sheer number of words must have included subject matter either not covered or only briefly covered in his New Testament epistles. Acts 19:8 tells us that he taught in one synagogue for "three months," and from Acts 19:10 we know that he taught in one location "daily" for two years. All this was oral teaching, probably including a lot of oral apostolic tradition, and common sense tells us a great deal of it was not recorded in Scripture.

If the Protestant says we are not bound to anything not found explicitly in Scripture, we might ask him where in Scripture we find such a notion, and why we should think ourselves in a better (or different) place than the earliest Christians, before the New Testament was compiled. Paul and the other apostles show no indication that pre-New Testament Christians were somehow in a less-prepared position regarding Christianity and Christian authority than we "Bible Christians" today are. If anything, the opposite is the case.

21. Authoritative oral tradition appears frequently in the New Testament

The Bible makes it clear in many passages that oral tradition is a legitimate, binding category of teaching.

1 Thessalonians 2:13: And we also thank God constantly for this, that when you received the word of God which you heard from us, you accepted it not as the word of men but as what it really is, the word of God, which is at work in you believers.

2 Timothy 1:13-14: Follow the pattern of the sound words which you have heard from me, in the faith and love which are in Christ Jesus; guard the truth that has been entrusted to you by the Holy Spirit who dwells within us.

2 Timothy 2:2: And what you have heard from me before many witnesses entrust to faithful men who will be able to teach others also.

1 John 1:5: This is the message we have heard from him and proclaim to you, that God is light and in him is no darkness at all.

1 John 2:24: Let what you heard from the beginning abide in you. If what you heard from the beginning abides in you, then you will abide in the Son and in the Father.

1 John 3:11: For this is the message which you have heard from the beginning, that we should love one another.

2 John 1:6: And this is love, that we follow his command-ments; this is the commandment, as you have heard from the beginning, that you follow love.

III.
Continuing Christian Adherence to Jewish (Pharisaical) Tradition and Mosaic Law

The broader, and rather important analogical argument that all the following sub-arguments or pieces of evidence in this section illustrate with cumulative force is this: By fully accepting Jewish Law and various Jewish traditions, Jesus and the apostles accepted the notions of, first, an ongoing binding, received Tradition that organically develops into subsequent Christian apostolic tradition and, secondly, the Jewish *paradigm of authority*, that itself always embraced *oral* as well as *written* Tradition.

Historic Protestant emphasis, to the contrary, tends to exaggerate the break between the old and new covenants or testaments, leading to a view suspicious of Jewish tradition and law and, by illogical extension, *all* tradition and law. This, in turn, leads to a tainting of the very category of "tradition" itself, even though Scripture distinguishes between good and bad tradition and sanctions good tradition (including oral tradition) as authoritative (as seen in argument No. 2 above).

In this somewhat indirect and subtle fashion, the following arguments constitute biblical evidence against *sola scriptura*. Acceptance of *authoritative, binding tradition* is fundamentally contrary to Scripture alone as the only binding and infallible rule of faith.

22. Jesus doesn't overturn or reject the Mosaic Law

He only modified it and taught a different application:

Matthew 5:17-20: Think not that I have come to abolish the law and the prophets; I have come not to abolish them but to fulfill them. For truly, I say to you, till heaven and earth pass away, not an iota, not a dot, will pass from the law until all is accomplished. Whoever then relaxes one of the least of these commandments and teaches men so, shall be called least in the kingdom of heaven; but he who does them and teaches them shall be called great in the kingdom of heaven. For I tell you, unless your righteousness exceeds that of the scribes and Pharisees, you will never enter the kingdom of heaven.

23. Jesus sanctions the extra-biblical tradition of "Moses' Seat"

Jewish tradition, including the extra-biblical Mishna, describes a sort of "teaching succession" from Moses on down.[9] Jesus acknowledges this tradition:

> Matthew 23:1-3: Then said Jesus to the crowds and to his disciples, "The scribes and the Pharisees sit on Moses' seat; so practice and observe whatever they tell you, but not what they do; for they preach, but do not practice.

Here, Jesus is sanctioning a tradition of pharisaical authority, and in so doing he is giving legitimacy to the concept of extra-biblical oral tradition. *Some* pharisaical traditions were corrupt (therefore Jesus condemned them, just as here he condemns their personal hypocrisy), but some were authoritative, so much so that even Jesus commands obedience to them.

24. Paul identifies himself as a Pharisee after his conversion, signifying a link to Jewish tradition

By stating, "according to the strictest party of our religion I have lived as a Pharisee" (Acts 26:5; cf. 23:6), Paul shows that he considered himself a Jew in good standing. In Philippians 3:5 he even calls himself a Pharisee, identifying himself with the party at the forefront of "rabbinic Judaism." He clearly wasn't thinking in terms of a clean break, or of two entirely distinct religions, as we do today.

25. Paul worships at synagogues

Paul even *presides* over the services in synagogues (Acts 13:13-44). Acts 18:4 describes Paul as having "argued in the synagogue every sabbath," implying that he was worshiping there, too. He wouldn't just barge in after the service and start arguing. It's very likely that he would have worshiped with them first (as he does, for example, in Acts 13, on the Sabbath day sitting down at the synagogue of Antioch in Pisidia).

26. Paul acknowledges the authority of the Jewish high priest Ananias

Paul saw himself as still under the authority of the Jewish high priest Ananias (Acts 23:1-8), as evidenced by his repentance for objecting to the latter's ordering him to be struck, and by his accompanying statement showing that he still believed the high priest a "ruler" of Christians—indeed, even a Christian apostle like himself. Ananias was a Sadducee, and by accounts a scoundrel, but Paul still thought he had authority, and shows him respect—even when Ananias was not dealing with matters pertaining strictly to the Old Testament and the Law.

Paul cites Exodus 22:28: "You shall not revile God, nor curse a ruler of your people." Now, why would he do that? Quite obviously, I think, he was applying it to *himself* (referring to his outburst recorded in 23:3). He says he didn't know it was the high priest, and we can take him at his word; if he had known it was the high priest he wouldn't have said what he did, because that would have gone against the injunction not to speak against a ruler of one's own people. It must, therefore, apply to himself; otherwise the saying makes no sense.

Thus, Paul is saying that the high priest is *his* ruler and that he is under his authority. It seems to be a straightforward, logical, deduction from the text. The continuing temple worship of Jesus and Paul and other early Christians clearly indicates that they recognized the authority of the Jewish priests in general; therefore, it would follow that they also recognized the *high* priest. Paul taught, after all, that even *secular* authorities should be respected and honored:

> Romans 13:1-7: Let every person be subject to the governing authorities. For there is no authority except from God, and those that exist have been instituted by God. Therefore he who resists the authorities resists what God has appointed, and those who resist will incur judgment. For rulers are not a terror to good conduct, but to bad. Would you have no fear of him who is in authority? Then do what is good, and you will receive his approval, for he is God's servant for your good. But if you do wrong, be afraid, for he does not bear the sword in vain; he is the servant of God to execute his wrath on the wrongdoer. Therefore one must be subject, not only to avoid God's wrath but also for the sake of conscience. For the same reason you also pay taxes, for the authorities are ministers of God, attending to this very thing. Pay all of them their dues, taxes to whom taxes are due, revenue to whom revenue is due, respect to whom respect is due, honor to whom honor is due.

Peter exhorted Christians to "be subject for the Lord's sake to every human institution, whether it be to the emperor as supreme" (1 Pet. 2:13), and to "honor the emperor" (2:17). This being the case, the early Christians would have respected the existing religious authority, and Paul's statement about the high priest indicates this. The *sola scriptura* position would not anticipate such an acknowledgment (thus, some Protestants, e.g., John Calvin, have argued that Paul was merely being sarcastic).

27. Jesus participates in the Old Testament sacrificial system

This is seen, for example, in his observance of the Passover ritual (Matt. 26:17-19; Mark 14:12-16; Luke 2:41-43; 22:7-15; John 2:13, 23; 13:1).

28. Jesus followed pharisaical traditions

Jesus adopted the pharisaical stand on controversial issues (Matt. 5:18-19; Luke 16:17), accepted the oral tradition of the academies, observed the proper mealtime procedures (Mark 6:56; Matt. 14:36), the Sabbath, and priestly regulations (Matt. 8:4; Mark 1:44; Luke 5:4).

29. Christians call Jews "brethren" and "fathers"

Christians refer to non-Christian Jews (Jews who practice Judaism and do not accept Jesus as Messiah) as "brethren" (Acts 13:26, 38; 22:1; 23:1, 5-6). St. Stephen, before a council of Jewish elders, scribes, and the high priest (Acts 6:12; 7:1) likewise addresses them as "brethren and fathers" (7:2). "Rulers of the synagogue" likewise refer to Paul and his companions as "brethren" (Acts 13:15).

30. The Galatians were even bigger hypocrites than the Pharisees

Paul said far worse of the Galatians and Corinthians than Jesus said of the Pharisees in Matthew 15 and 23 and elsewhere. Yet, he continued to regard them as brothers in Christ and as a "church." Therefore, Jesus could have criticized the Pharisees and yet still respected them and their traditions. Nicodemus and Joseph of Arimathea were righteous Pharisees. Jesus was even buried in the latter's tomb.

31. Caiaphas the high priest "prophesied"

Such a (surprising) proclamation of truth can only be inspired by the Holy Spirit:

> John 11:49-52: But one of them, Ca'iaphas, who was high priest that year, said to them, "You know nothing at all; you do not understand that it is expedient for you that one man

should die for the people, and that the whole nation should not perish." He did not say this of his own accord, but being high priest that year he prophesied that Jesus should die for the nation, and not for the nation only, but to gather into one the children of God who are scattered abroad.

Caiaphas is connected with Old Testament tradition, insofar as the category of high priest was in accordance with Mosaic Law and the sacrificial system. Thus, his office is a remnant of that "old" system, which is not rejected by Jesus and the apostles, as we have seen throughout this section.

32. Christianity adopted late pharisaical traditions and doctrines

Early Christianity accepted and developed extra-biblical doctrines of Pharisaical Judaism; for example, resurrection, the soul, the afterlife, eternal reward or damnation, angelology and demonology (all notions rejected by the Sadducees). The Old Testament taught very little about these things, and only primitively. But the apocalyptic literature of the Jews had a lot to say about them. Christianity presupposed and utilized this non-biblical literature in its own doctrinal development.

This is not to dispute that *revelation* was the primary source of Christian doctrine. The early Church received its teaching from Jesus and the apostles; it did not merely warm over Jewish traditions it happened to agree with. But we note that there is a direct development from the old covenant to the new, including incorporation of theological ideas from the late period of Judaism after the time of the completion of all or almost all of the Old Testament.

33. The Sadducees were the "liberals" and *sola scriptura* advocates of their time

If the Pharisees and their tradition were in many ways the forerunners of Christian theology, the Sadducees were the proto-heretics. (Tellingly, Christian Pharisees are referred to in Acts 15:5 and Philippians 3:5, but the Bible never mentions Christian Sadducees.) In addition to denying the soul and the afterlife, the Sadducees also rejected all authoritative oral teaching, and essentially believed in *sola scriptura*. Fortunately, neither the (orthodox) Old Testament Jews nor the early Church followed the Sadducees in their heretical ideas.

It would be impossible to be a Sadducee *and* a Christian, since the former rejected non-negotiable doctrines that all Christians must believe, most notably resurrection (how can one believe in the resurrection of Jesus without believing in resurrection, period?), whereas one can be simultaneously a Christian and a Pharisee. Thus, Paul calls himself one (Acts 23:6; 26:5), Jesus continues their traditions (see No. 28), and no one is ever called a Christian Sadducee in Scripture.

34. Christians continued temple worship and participation in sacrifices

Acts 3:1 tells us that Peter and John were worshiping at the temple, and Acts 2:46 describes the early Christians as "day by day, attending the temple together."

This would have certainly included Paul, too, when he was in Jerusalem; he himself alludes to his presence in the temple as well as synagogues (Acts 24:12), and is described as continuing to participate in temple rituals (Acts 21:26: "Then Paul took the men, and the next day he purified himself with them and went into the temple, to give notice when the days of purification would be fulfilled and the offering presented for every one of them"). In Acts 22:17 he refers to his practice of "praying in the temple," and in Acts 24:18 as having been "purified in the temple" (see also 24:17: "I came to bring to my nation alms and offerings").

35. Ancient Judaism is analogous to and was developed by Catholicism, not Protestantism

It is hardly possible to make an analogy between the ancient Jewish authority structure and Protestantism. In the former, oral tradition was central from the beginning, and flourished even more after the canon of the Old Testament was finalized. At that point, the (mostly oral) methods and traditions that later crystallized into the written Talmud intensified and continued unabated for another six centuries. After that, Judaism continued to discuss and comment on the Talmud itself, and does to this day. The comparison to Catholicism is much more apt:

A) Oral law in Judaism corresponds to oral tradition in the New Testament (e.g., 2 Timothy 1:13-14; 2:2) and Catholic tradition.

B) In its interpretive and developmental aspects, Jewish oral law is similar to Catholic development of dogma and the historical growth of conciliar and magisterial teaching.

C) Many Jews believed (and some still do) that the "oral Torah" went back to Moses on Mount Sinai, and ultimately to God, and was received simultaneously with the written Torah. Likewise, Catholics believe that Catholic tradition was received simultaneously from the apostles—who received it from Jesus—with the "gospel," which was eventually formulated into the New Testament.

Any affinity between the Judaism of Jesus' time and *sola scriptura* is impossible to maintain, since the Jews accepted the oral Torah as equally authoritative, the canon of the Old Testament was only gradually formed (the Pentateuch alone was authoritatively collected 500 years after David), and authoritative and binding talmudic speculation and interpretation flourished even after the Old Testament had been completed and organized (a few centuries after Christ).

Most Protestants deny even an authoritative and binding *apostolic* (let alone Jewish) tradition, since this notion runs counter to the definition of *sola scriptura*. Some Protestants argue that the Old Testament religious system is closer in spirit to Protestantism, but in order to do so they must deny that the ancient Jews ever accepted authoritative oral tradition (thus assuming the position of the Sadducees, who held to "Torah alone").

IV.
Prophecy and Proclamation: "Word of God" and "Word of the Lord"

36. "Word of the Lord" and "Word of God" are not usually references to Scripture

In the Bible, the phrases "Word of God" or "Word of the Lord" are by no means restricted to the meaning of "Bible" or "Scripture," or even any writing at all. This is especially obvious in the case of the prophets.

2 Samuel 7:4-5: But that same night the word of the LORD came to Nathan, "Go and tell my servant David, 'Thus says the LORD: Would you build me a house to dwell in?'"

1 Kings 12:22-24: But the word of God came to Shemai'ah the man of God: "Say to Rehobo'am the son of Solomon, king of Judah, and to all the house of Judah and Benjamin, and to the rest of the people, 'Thus says the LORD, You shall not go up or fight against your kinsmen the people of Israel. Return every man to his home, for this thing is from me.'" So they hearkened to the word of the LORD, and went home again, according to the word of the LORD.

1 Kings 14:18: According to the word of the LORD, which he spoke by his servant Ahi'jah the prophet.

1 Kings 17:16: According to the word of the LORD which he spoke by Eli'jah.

Jeremiah 25:3: For twenty-three years, from the thirteenth year of Josi'ah the son of Amon, king of Judah, to this day, the word of the LORD has come to me, and I have spoken persistently to you, but you have not listened.

Those expressions are used to describe verbal, oratorical proclamation in the New Testament as well:

Matthew 13:19: When any one hears the word of the kingdom.

Luke 5:1: While the people pressed upon him to hear the word of God, he was standing by the lake of Gennes'aret (cf. 3:2-3).

Luke 11:28: But he said, "Blessed rather are those who hear the word of God and keep it!" (cf. 8:10-21).

Acts 4:31: And when they had prayed, the place in which they were gathered together was shaken; and they were all filled with the Holy Spirit and spoke the word of God with boldness.

Acts 6:2: And the Twelve summoned the body of the disciples and said, "It is not right that we should give up preaching the word of God to serve tables."

Acts 8:25: Now when they had testified and spoken the word of the Lord, they returned to Jerusalem, preaching the gospel to many villages of the Samaritans (cf. 11:1; 12:24; 13:5, 7, 44, 46, 48-49; 14:3; 15:7, 35-36; 16:32; 17:15; 18:11; 19:10, 20; 20:32).

Acts 15:35: But Paul and Barnabas remained in Antioch, teaching and preaching the word of the Lord, with many others also.

Romans 10:8: The word is near you, on your lips and in your heart (that is, the word of faith which we preach).

Ephesians 1:13: In him you also, who have heard the word of truth, the gospel of your salvation.

Philippians 1:14: Much more bold to speak the word of God without fear (cf. 2:16).

1 Thessalonians 1:8: The word of the Lord sounded forth from you in Macedo'nia and Acha'ia.

1 Thessalonians 2:13: You received the word of God, which you heard from us (cf. Acts 8:5-6, 14).

Hebrews 1:7: Remember your leaders, those who spoke to you the word of God.

Hebrews 11:3: By faith we understand that the world was created by the word of God, so that what is seen was made out of things which do not appear (cf. 2 Pet. 3:5; John 1:1, 14; Rev. 19:13).

1 Peter 1:25: "But the word of the Lord abides forever." That word is the good news which was preached to you.

There are many more instances of (non-written) "word" in which it is implied to mean "word of God" (e.g., Matt. 4:4; Luke 4:32; John 8:31, 37, 43, 51-52; 17:20; many times in Acts; Gal. 6:6; Col. 4:3; 2 Tim. 4:2; James 1:22-23; 1 John 2:7).

37. Oral prophecy was an ongoing New Testament charism

Prophecy was common in apostolic times (Acts 2:18). The Ephesians did it (Acts 19:6), as did the daughters of Philip (Acts 21:9), and the Corinthians (1 Cor. 11:4-5). There were even prophets (in terms of a calling or office), in addition to folks who prophesied on occasion. In 1 Corinthians 14, Paul repeatedly teaches about prophesying.

Prophets were listed in lists of ministries (1 Cor. 12:28-29; Eph. 4:11) and worked with teachers, as in Antioch (Acts 13:1). They both proclaimed and predicted (see, e.g., Agabus: Acts 11:28; 21:10-11). Prophets exhorted believers (Acts 15:32) and provided edification (1 Cor. 14:3). Prophecy is described as *rev-*

elation (1 Cor. 14:30) and as connected with the Holy Spirit (plausible implication of 1 Thessalonians 5:19-20). Prophets were subject to the norm of New Testament or apostolic tradition (1 Cor. 14:29, 37-38), just as the Old Testament prophets had to be in conformity with the Law of Moses.

Obviously, only a small percentage of the oral utterances of these many prophets, just as with those of the apostles and evangelists (and Jesus, for that matter), could make their way into the New Testament. But they possessed a measure of authority all the same.

38. Tradition and Scripture both derive from the larger category of "word of God"

The Protestant claims that (true, authentic) tradition is simply the gospel message, which is fully contained in the New Testament. It is Scripture itself. But the Bible never states this. The Bible does indeed equate "tradition" and "word of God" and "gospel." But as we saw earlier, the biblical phrase "word of God" means more than "written Scripture"—it also refers to oral utterances. In its broadest biblical sense, then, it is a larger category of authoritative statements inspired or at least directly guided by God, from which both oral tradition and written Scripture flow.

Therefore, the Second Vatican Council's *Dei Verbum* reflects the biblical outlook on authority when it speaks of Scripture and Tradition "flowing from the same divine wellspring." (II:9) Protestantism deviates from the Bible in equating tradition with written Scripture and denying a larger "word of God" that lies behind both.

39. In his epistles to the Thessalonians, Paul frequently references tradition but rarely alludes to Scripture

Contrary to the claims of some Protestants, Paul never urges his readers to "test all truth-claims by Scripture" in 2 Thessalonians. There "gospel" is mentioned twice (1:8 and 2:14) and "tradition" twice (2:15 and 3:6), but neither "Scripture" nor "scriptures" appears. "Word of the Lord" appears once (3:1—"Finally, brethren, pray for us, that the word of the Lord may speed on and triumph, as it did among you"), but it appears not to refer to the Bible. Rather, it refers to the proclamation of the gospel: the story of Jesus' death on the cross on our behalf, his resurrection, ascension, and atonement, and the redemption. Proclaiming this gospel is what Paul and his aides were doing, not going around passing out Bibles.

A similar state of affairs occurs in 1 Thessalonians. "Scripture" or "scriptures" never appears. "Word," "word of the Lord," and "word of God" appear five times (1:6, 8; 2:13; 4:15), but clearly in the sense of oral proclamation, not written Scripture. We have no reason from the text to believe that this oral "word of the Lord" was understood to be restricted to what was later recorded in the New Testament.

V.
The Alleged Perspicuity of Scripture and the Necessity of Authoritative Interpretation

40. Minimalistic Christianity is not the biblical norm

If a man was stranded on a desert island with nothing but a Bible, I believe he could be saved (that is, go to heaven—whether he'd make it off the island is another matter). It wouldn't be absolutely necessary to have a Church or Tradition. For that matter, he could be saved without a Bible, or without ever having heard a word of it, as long as he sought truth; for God said his existence is evident from the things he made (see Romans 1). This does not disprove, however, the need for a Church and an authoritative Tradition (and a written Scripture) in normal circumstances.

That would be like saying, "I *could* live on nothing but bread and water, with no plumbing, medicine, or modern conveniences, therefore those things aren't important." Sure, maybe you could, but that's not the best or healthiest way to live. God does not want us to spiritually handicap ourselves; rather, he wants us to take advantage of all the guides to truth he has provided—including the Church and Tradition—to help us better follow the path of discipleship.

41. The historical wisdom of the Church is a better interpreter of Scripture than any individual or denomination

Protestants grant to individuals the authority to decide (presumably by the illumination of the Holy Spirit) what is true and what isn't, while denying it to the Church. This makes no sense. If Protestants discount the Church's binding authority because the Church is made of fallible, sinful men, then they have to discount every individual's interpretation, since each person is a fallible sinner, too!

There is no preexisting hermeneutical grid to which Protestants can appeal when they profess "Scripture alone" over

Church and Tradition. Every man is on his own, his interpretations subject to error like any other fallible man's. Of
what use, then, is an ostensibly infallible Scripture? Practically
speaking, the Bible can be no more infallible than our own
contradictory interpretations of it.

Faced with the divisions and contradictions that inevitably flow from *sola scriptura* (the denominational problem),
Protestants are forced to appeal to one of two equally unsatis-
factory solutions:

A) Claim that their own brand of Protestantism is the true
one to be believed above all others. This was the standard
approach taken by the Reformers and virtually all the early
Protestant factions. But since they denied apostolic succession as historically understood, the appeal to one's own
truth was arbitrary and ahistorical.

B) Pretend that doctrines over which Protestants disagree
(almost all doctrines other than those on which they agree
with Catholics) are "secondary" and not important enough
to fight over in order to arrive at and determine truth in
those matters. This leads to relativizing a host of doctrines,
and a gradual loss of fidelity even to primary teachings.

Since both "solutions" are unbiblical, illogical, and imprac-
tical, Protestants must assert that the Bible supports denominationalism and an "invisible Church" ecclesiology, and either
that history and apostolicity don't matter, or that Protestantism is actually the true heir to historical Christianity—having cast off the alleged corruptions of the apostate medieval
Church and restored the true, biblical faith. Certain Reformed
Protestants today are choosing that second option, since they
care about apostolicity and agree with us that Christianity is
an inherently historical religion. But that takes them back to
the burden of making a biblical case for any brand of Protestant

ecclesiology, and of showing a consistent identification with the historical Church, for which there is no evidence.

42. False assumptions can lead biblical exegetes astray, but the Church is a sure guide

The Bible is a book, and like other books it must be interpreted. Whether it is clear or obscure in its meanings is a separate issue. In fact, Catholics don't think it is so much obscure or mysterious as it is prone to distorted interpretations. We don't believe that every passage is an utter mystery, riddle, and enigma (to paraphrase Churchill's description of Russia). Where it is more difficult to interpret correctly, the difficulty is compounded by readers' false theological presuppositions, selective prooftexting, neglect of context, unbridled private judgment, disregard for exegetical and doctrinal precedent, and so on. Such common tendencies tell against *sola scriptura*, and point to a need for an authoritative teaching and interpreting Church.

It is not that Scripture is an indecipherable code that only Holy Mother Church can break. Rather, the Church speaks authoritatively as to what Holy Scripture *teaches*, just as it spoke authoritatively as to which books belonged in the canon of Scripture. In both instances, Scripture is inherently what it is: God's inspired, inerrant, written revelation. But sinful mankind's predilection to disunity of belief made the teaching Church absolutely necessary.

43. The Bible itself teaches that it can be misinterpreted

Scripture doesn't have to be perfectly clear—not if it was always intended by God to be understood within an overall context of Church and Tradition. Thus, the Bible can say that interpretation of Scripture (in this case, prophecies found in Scripture) is not "a matter of one's own interpretation" (2 Pet. 1:20) because it comes from God, not men (v. 21). Moreover, it warns that erroneous interpretation of difficult parts of the Bible can lead people astray:

> 2 Peter 3:15-17: So also our beloved brother Paul wrote to you according to the wisdom given him, speaking of this as he does in all his letters. There are some things in them hard to understand, which the ignorant and unstable twist to their own destruction, as they do the other scriptures.

44. Perspicuity and denominationalism are at odds

Some Protestants argue that Psalms 19:7 and 119:130 inform us that the Word of God can be grasped by the simple. There is a significant sense in which this is indeed true. But then, if it were true in a formal sense, why such doctrinal confusion in Protestantism? One of Protestantism's insuperable problems is that in the endeavor to show that Scripture is perspicuous, it merely heightens and magnifies the folly of denominationalism and competing truth claims.

Theoretically, each Protestant can come up with a radically new brand of Christianity if he so chooses. He can start a new denomination. He can declare that historical precedents for doctrines x, y, and z are hopelessly corrupt and "unbiblical" and discard them at will—even, in extreme cases, doing so with full knowledge that virtually all the Fathers or the entire history of Christianity between Jesus and the year 1517 held something quite otherwise. No one can deny this is possible because it is precisely what Luther and Calvin, the founders of the very system, themselves did.

Catholics happily acknowledge that Protestants can and do arrive at a great deal of truth by *sola scriptura,* because the Bible is truth. But when groups of Protestants get something wrong, they have no way of correcting the error or even *knowing* that it is wrong, and have to adopt theological pluralism and tolerance of contradiction. This is not good. The devil is the father of lies. Where contradiction is, that is not the Spirit of Truth.

45. Protestantism is radically contradictory in how it harmonizes and systematizes "plain" Scripture

Protestants say that the committed, regenerate layman can understand perspicuous Scripture, and that by comparing Bible passages the truth can always be found. But there are different *ways* of comparing and harmonizing Bible passages. There is the Calvinist way and the Arminian way and the Baptist way; there are the Lutheran, Anglican, Nazarene, Presbyterian, Methodist, and Plymouth Brethren ways; the Seventh-Day Adventist, Mennonite, Church of God, and Church of Christ ways, and so on.

More sophisticated proponents of *sola scriptura* often attempt to nuance and qualify internal Protestant difficulties by referring to denominational traditions and teachers so as to avoid association with the obvious deficiencies of private interpretation. But think about it: How can this work if the individual isn't personally familiar with the Bible? How can he simply accept the authority of various Bible teachers and denominational traditions (which are merely accumulations of teachings over time) to give him the truth about the Bible? How is that preferable to accepting what the Church has already passed down?

Instead of believing in an infallible Church, protected and guided by the Holy Spirit, now the individual has to wade through competing Protestant interpretations and traditions and subjectively, fallibly, choose one tradition as his own—what he privately judges to be the "most biblical" one. This is a recipe for disaster. And the history of Protestantism has borne this out.

46. The Bible teaches that biblical interpretation is necessary

It doesn't follow that because interpretation exists, Scripture is "subject to it" in the sense that it is inferior. That is an unbiblical and false Protestant dichotomy. To say that authoritative Scripture has to be interpreted is not to denigrate it in the slightest. Interpretation *must* exist because that is simply the reality for all written documents, even inspired ones. This is, in fact, presupposed in Scripture itself. In addition to 2 Peter 1:20 and 3:15-17:

> Mark 4:33-34: With many such parables he spoke the word to them, as they were able to hear it; he did not speak to them without a parable, but privately to his own disciples he explained everything.

> Acts 8:28-31: He was reading the prophet Isaiah. And the Spirit said to Philip, "Go up and join this chariot." So Philip ran to him, and heard him reading Isaiah the prophet, and asked, "Do you understand what you are reading?" And he said, "How can I, unless someone guides me?" And he invited Philip to come up and sit with him.

> 2 Peter 3:15-16: Paul wrote to you according to the wisdom given him . . . in all his letters. There are some things in them hard to understand, which the ignorant and unstable twist to their destruction.

47. Jesus reveals hard Bible truths to the disciples at Emmaus

The two disciples on the road to Emmaus marveled at how Jesus "opened to us the Scriptures" (Luke 24:32). In other words, they didn't understand those prophecies until Jesus explained them and showed how they were fulfilled. Thus, Old Testament Scripture was insufficient for these messianic truths to be grasped simply by reading them.

One could reply that the Jews were hard-hearted, or that they lacked the Holy Spirit and God's grace to illuminate their understanding. But that proves too much, because it would also have to apply to these two disciples, and indeed to all of the disciples, who did not understand what was happening even *after* Jesus repeatedly told them that he was to suffer and to die, and that this was all foretold. They didn't "get it" until after he was crucified.

48. Sincere study alone does not guarantee correct interpretation of Scripture

Some Protestants would contend that erroneous and contradictory interpretations flow from ignorance and insufficient study, and that those who study the Bible in great depth will tend to agree on its central teachings. But that's simply not true. Jehovah's Witnesses and Mormons know their Bible well (of course they have horrendous hermeneutical principles, as well as flawed translations), and they can't even arrive at basic truths about the Trinitarian nature of God and the divinity of Christ. Calvin and Luther both knew the Bible inside out, yet they disagreed on a host of things (baptismal regeneration, Eucharist, et cetera). The argument doesn't fly.

The history of Protestant sectarianism suggests that the problem isn't lack of knowledge but the lack of a biblical authority structure (Church, Bible, Tradition: the "three-legged stool") and flawed premises (*sola scriptura*, private judgment, supremacy of the individual conscience, competing ecclesiologies) that are based neither on Scripture nor Tradition but on erroneous "traditions of men."

49. *Sola scriptura* means it's always the other guy's problem

In a variation of the "ignorance" argument above, if the "other guy" disagrees with me it is (under Protestant principles) because I have studied Scripture and its interpretation more than he has, or because the Holy Spirit is guiding me and not him—perhaps because of some sin or lack of faith on his part, or an unwillingness to go "where God leads him." Working on the premise that Scripture is always clear, where there is disagreement I always have to accuse the other person of some deficiency.

Catholics, on the other hand, simply say a person is mistaken when he disagrees with the history of Christian doctrine, passed down in an unbroken chain from the apostles and safeguarded by the Church. Certain teachings were received from Jesus, and they are true. What the biblical arguments supporting them may be is another issue. But they are true because Jesus passed them down, and Christians believed them (and were justified in doing so) even before biblical arguments could be produced.

50. The Bible never lists its "essential" teachings

Protestants might agree that some things in Scripture are difficult to understand unaided but contend that the *essential* teachings of Scripture are clear to all who read while seeking God's guidance and to those who are willing to live by what they learn in the Bible. But what *are* the "essential" teachings? Who has the authority to determine that? According to *sola scriptura*, the answer must be found in Scripture itself. Where in the Bible is a list of such teachings? It doesn't exist.

Catholics largely agree that the Bible is accessible, that its essential teachings are understandable to those with an open heart and mind; however, both Scripture and the history of mankind tell us that that the human heart is "deceitful above all things" (Jer. 17:9). All the more reason, then, why it made sense for God to provide his people with an authoritative Church to guide them, not only where Scripture's meaning is tricky but also where it plainly spells out essential teachings.

51. The Bible asserts that its teachings have to be "opened"

In Luke 24:32, the two disciples on the road to Emmaus marveled at how Jesus "opened to us the scriptures." The Greek word for "opened" is *dianoigo* (Strong's word #1272). According to Joseph Thayer's *Greek-English Lexicon of the New Testament,* it means "to open by dividing or drawing asunder, to open thoroughly (what had been closed)." This meaning can be seen in other passages where *dianoigo* appears (Mark 7:34-35; Luke 2:23; 24:31, 45; Acts 16:14; 17:3).

Here, Scripture itself appears to be informing us that some parts of it were "closed" and "not plain" until the infallible teaching authority and interpretation of our Lord Jesus opened it up and made it plain. This runs utterly contrary to the Protestant notion of perspicuity of Scripture and its more or less ubiquitous self-interpreting nature.

52. Some things in the Gospels are difficult to understand: John 6, for example

Jesus' teaching on the Eucharist in John 6 scandalized many of his disciples. "This is a hard saying; who can listen to it?" (6:60). In 6:66 we learn that this inability to understand (or accept) caused disciples to stop following Jesus, the only time we ever see that in Scripture.

Now, if some of Jesus' very *disciples* couldn't understand what he said to them face to face, doesn't it follow that some reading it *today* might very well not understand either? John's gospel demonstrates that authoritative interpretation is necessary. Jesus' own preaching caused confusion and division among his disciples; those same words as recorded in Scripture do likewise when left to individual interpretation, for the Bible is neither completely clear nor self-interpreting.

The same would apply, for that matter, to the entire gospel story of Jesus' life and death, because his own disciples didn't grasp what was going on (with Jesus even saying at one point that Satan was speaking through Peter). If they didn't get it—they who knew Jesus when he walked on Earth—what of the millions who would read about the story afterward?

53. In the Old Covenant, authoritative teaching authority was constantly exercised

The Catholic rule of faith (the "three-legged stool" of Scrip-ture-Church-Tradition) is analogous to the rule of faith for the ancient Jews, who believed in the authoritative interpretation of their Torah and, eventually, the Old Testament as a whole:

- Exodus 18:20: Moses was to teach the Jews the "statutes and the decisions"—not just read them. Since he was the lawgiver and author of the Torah, it stands to reason that his interpretation and teaching would be authoritative.
- Leviticus 10:11: Moses' brother, Aaron, is also command-ed by God to teach.
- Deuteronomy 17:8-13: The levitical priests had binding authority in legal matters (derived from the Torah itself). They interpreted the biblical injunctions (17:11). The pen-alty for disobedience was death (17:12), since the offender didn't obey "the priest who stands to minister there be-fore the LORD your God." (Cf. Deuteronomy 19:16-17; 2 Chronicles 19:8-10.)
- Deuteronomy 24:8: Levitical priests had the final say and authority (in this instance, in the case of leprosy). This was a matter of Jewish law.
- Deuteronomy 33:10: Levite priests were to teach Israel the ordinances and law. (Cf. 2 Chronicles 15:3; Malachi 2:6-8—The latter calls them "messenger of the LORD of hosts".)
- Ezra 7:6,10: Ezra, a priest and scribe, studied the Law and taught it to Israel. His authority was binding, under pain of imprisonment, banishment, loss of goods, and even death (7:25-26).
- Nehemiah 8:1-8: Ezra reads the Law of Moses to the people in Jerusalem (8:3). In 8:7 we find thirteen Levites who assisted Ezra and "helped the people to understand the law." Much earlier, in King Jehoshaphat's reign, we find Levites exercising the same function (2 Chron. 17:8-9). Neither *sola scriptura* nor the concept of "perspicuity" appears here.

- Nehemiah 8:8: They read from the book, from the Law of God, clearly (or with "interpretation"), and they gave the sense, so that the people understood the reading. So, the people did indeed understand the law (8:12), but not without much assistance after hearing it.

The Old Testament and Jewish history attest to a fact Catholics assert against *sola scriptura* and Protestantism: Scripture requires an authoritative interpreter. To be authoritative it has to come from Jesus himself. This is the Church, with a binding tradition transmitted to us by Christ through the apostles.

Jewish scholars themselves confirm that this was indeed the case in ancient Israel, and they utilize the Bible to do it (even using some of the same prooftexts), just as I did above. For example, in the "Priests" entry in the *Jewish Encyclopedia* of 1906 we read:

"Whosoever had to consult God went out to the tent of meeting," where Moses ascertained the will of God; and just as Moses, in his capacity of priest, was the intermediary through whom Yhwh revealed the Torah to the Israelites in the wilderness, and through whom His judgment was invoked in all difficult cases, such as could not be adjusted without reference to this highest tribunal (Ex. xviii. 16 *et seq.*), so the priests, down to the close of pre-exilic times, were the authoritative interpreters of the Law, while the sanctuaries were the seats of judgment.

Thus the Book of the Covenant prescribes that all dubious criminal cases "be brought before God," that is, be referred to Him by the priest for decision (Ex. xxii.7, 8). . . . The Blessing of Moses proves that the sacred lots continued to be cast by the priests during the time of the monarchy, inasmuch as it speaks of the urim and thummim as insignia of the priesthood (Deut. xxxiii. 8). This document shows, as does also the Deuteronomic code, that throughout pre-exilic times the expounding of the Torah and the administration of justice remained the specific functions of the priests. It declares that the priests are the guardians of God's teachings and Law, and that it is their mission to teach God's judgments and Torah to Israel (Deut. xxxiii. 9, 10), while the Deuteronomic code decrees that all difficult criminal as well as civil cases be referred to the priests (*ib.* xvii. 8-11, xxi. 5). Further proof to the same effect lies in the frequent references of the Prophets to the judicial and teaching functions of the priesthood (comp. Amos ii. 8; Hos. iv. 6; Isa. xxviii. 7; Micah iii. 11; Jer. ii. 8, xviii. 18; Ezek. vii. 26).[10]

VI.
General or Miscellaneous Arguments
Relating to *Sola Scriptura*

54. The Bible never teaches that oral tradition would cease and *sola scriptura* become the new rule of faith

Some Protestants argue that once the canon was established, oral traditions ended and *sola scriptura* became the rule of faith. Reformed Baptist apologist James R. White provides a typical example:

> While it [1 Corinthians 11:23] does illustrate the reality that for a time the early Christians were dependent on the transmissions of this information in an oral manner, it does not logically follow that God intended Christians to *always* remain dependent in this way. Nor does it provide support for the idea that Paul taught the Christians things that, while important for salvation and proper belief, are nowhere recorded for us in Scripture. Instead, we find passages that indicate a harmony and identity between the preaching of the Apostles and their written epistles and gospels. . . .
>
> Often the Apostles indicate that they are repeating in written form what they taught orally.[11]

Catholics agree that oral apostolic tradition must be and always *is* in harmony with Scripture; we deny, however, that it is *identical* in minute content with the words in the Bible. White gives 2 Thessalonians 2:5 and 2 Peter 1:12-15 as examples of his view that the two are synonymous. The latter passage doesn't prove what he contends, not even partially. Peter writes that he wants to "remind" his followers of Christian teaching, never saying specifically that he means by *writing* (let alone by writing Scripture only). In fact, in 2:13 he states, "I think it right, as long as I am in this body, to arouse you by way of reminder."

That's an odd way to describe a piece of writing, which would endure beyond a person's death. It's more plausible to interpret it as his wanting to teach them in person, orally. He never hints at the Protestant myth that is the topic of this section.

The larger problem is that White can't logically or exegetically jump from individual instances of the written word's reaffirming oral teaching to a universal rule of faith whereby written Scripture alone is authoritative.

Indeed, if the latter were truly the case, why wouldn't Scripture itself *say* so, and in a way that was perfectly clear and logically coherent within a *sola scriptura* paradigm? In the absence of such a statement, Protestants must appeal to a man-made tradition—the idea that after 400 years of Christianity *sola scriptura* would suddenly become the new rule of faith (voiding all previous authoritative extra-biblical apostolic tradition)—to establish the principle that undergirds their entire theology.

Protestants say that the Bible is the "sole final and infallible authority," yet the very notion has to be superimposed on it from without. We have a word for that: *eisegesis*, literally, "reading into" the biblical text one's predispositions.

55. The very nature of *sola scriptura* requires it to be explicitly found in the Bible itself

Given *sola scriptura*'s central premise, the Protestant has no choice but to prove that the Bible clearly and explicitly teaches the principle. Yet he cannot, because the Bible does not. What it *does* explicitly teach is the infallible, binding authority of Tradition (2 Thess. 2:15; 3:6; Phil. 4:9; 2 Tim. 1:13-14; 2:2; and many more) and of the Church (Acts 15:1-32; 16:4; 20:28; 1 Tim. 3:15). Moreover, the Bible—in its indications of binding tradition, authoritative oral tradition, apostolic succession, strong Church authority, the papacy, Holy Spirit-led councils, et cetera—flat-out contradicts *sola scriptura* but not Catholic doctrines revealed through Tradition (such as the Assumption of Mary).

Why is it required of Catholics, then, to provide more scriptural "proof" for doctrines such as the Assumption or an infallible papacy than Protestants are required to give for *sola scriptura*? For if ever a tradition needed to be incontrovertibly grounded in plain biblical teaching, it is that one.

56. Scripture alone may be sufficient for many doctrines, but not all

One can arrive at a great number of true doctrines by reading Scripture alone. I did. Before I became Catholic I had arrived at maybe seventy percent of Catholic doctrines just on the authority of the Bible. And most other Catholic doctrines, once they were explained to me, did not strike me as unbiblical.

The problem comes when the Calvinist down the block denies baptismal regeneration, while his Lutheran brother affirms it. It's with the Baptist two houses down, who believes in adult baptism only, contradicting both his Calvinist and Lutheran brethren, who adhere to infant baptism (while differing on its effects). And with the Presbyterian or broad Anglican who denies the Real Presence of Christ in the Eucharist, while his fellow *sola scriptura*-adhering Lutherans and traditional Anglicans accept it.

And on it goes, with any number of examples of incoherence and contradiction that Protestants are inherently burdened with. All these Protestants are operating on the principle of Scripture alone, just as did the ancient Arians and virtually all heretics.

57. The Trinity was an early test case for Tradition versus *sola scriptura*

One of Christianity's most essential doctrines, the Trinitarian nature of God, is a perfect test case for the limits of Scripture's perspicuity and thus for the need for extra-biblical authority.

Catholics and Protestants can agree that the doctrine is contained, to one degree or another, in the Bible. Yet that hasn't stopped heretics and sectarians, both ancient and modern, from denying it based on *their reading of Scripture.*

This is why the Church Fathers who opposed the Arians (who denied the divinity of Christ and thus the Trinity) in the fourth century appealed to Scripture in their arguments, but then concluded by appealing to the Church and apostolic tradition. They could say, "The Church has taught the Holy Trinity all the way back to the beginning; therefore it is true, because the Church is protected by the Holy Spirit, and the teaching goes back to Jesus and the apostles." But the Arians had no such history they could produce, so they had to fall back on Bible alone; to bogus prooftexts that Jesus was created.

Four short excerpts from St. Athanasius, the heroic fourth-century opponent of the Arian heretics who is beloved by many Protestants (probably second in that respect only to St. Augustine), more than suffice to illustrate how he—like the Church Fathers in general—approached the issue of misinterpretations of Scripture and heresy:

> However here too they introduce their private fictions, and contend that the Son and the Father are not in such wise "one," or "like," as the Church preaches, but as they themselves would have it. (*Discourse Against the Arians*, III, 3:10)

> Inventors of unlawful heresies, who indeed refer to the Scriptures, but do not hold such opinions as the saints have handed down, and receiving them as the traditions of men, err. (Festal Letter 2:6)

> See, we are proving that this view has been transmitted from father to father; but ye, O modern Jews and disciples of Caiaphas, how many fathers can ye assign to your phrases? (*Defense of the Nicene Definition*, 27)

For, what our Fathers have delivered, this is truly doctrine. (*De Decretis* 4)

58. Church and Scripture are not a zero-sum game

Protestants tend think in dichotomous terms—for example, grace as opposed to nature, justification as opposed to sanctification. So, for them to accept binding Church authority is somehow to "abandon the standard of Scripture," as if it were a zero-sum game where Scripture is the air in a glass and the Church is the water added to the glass. In this mindset, the more water ("Church") is added, the less Scripture there can be, so that a full glass of "the Church" leaves no room for the Bible at all as the "standard." None of this is Catholic teaching and neither does it logically follow from the notion of Church authority. It's a false dilemma and a false dichotomy.

Scripture, however, bolsters the Catholic "both/and" way of thinking. Examine Paul's use of the term "Scripture" or "word of God" (when it refers clearly to Scripture), along with citations of Old Testament Scripture, compared to his use of "Church" (in a non-local sense) or "Body," as well as "tradition" and its equivalents. He makes frequent use of all three as authoritative.

We find, looking closely, that Paul relies on the "three-legged stool" of Scripture-Church-Tradition. In 1 Corinthians, for example, he refers to or cites Scripture twenty times, alludes to the Church in some fashion eleven times, and "tradition" in some manner eight times. He regards all as authoritative for the Christian. In his epistle to the Colossians, he mentions the concepts of Church and tradition six times each, but Scripture not at all (something that could not be accepted, I submit, under the *sola scriptura* paradigm). Paul's revealing (and very "Catholic") use of the three concepts will be explored in greater depth in No. 60 below.

59. In Ephesians 4, Paul shows no awareness of a *sola scriptura* rule of faith

Protestants contend that Scripture is the rule of faith; the only infallible authority for theological truth. If that were the case, it stands to reason that in a Bible passage talking about truth over and over again, denouncing falsehood, and referring to "one faith" and "the unity of faith," Scripture ought to be mentioned.

If *sola scriptura* were true, Ephesians 4 would be a logical and likely place for Paul to reiterate that Scripture is the rule of faith. But he doesn't. He does refer repeatedly to truth and denounces falsehood, but instead of Scripture he refers to the *Church* over and over—to the "one body" with its various ecclesial offices (italics mine):

> Ephesians 4:4-6, 11-16, 21-25: There is *one body* and one Spirit, just as you were called to the one hope that belongs *to your call*, one Lord, one faith, one baptism, one God and Father of us all, who is above all and through all and in all. . . . And *his gifts* were that some should be *apostles, some prophets, some evangelists, some pastors and teachers*, to equip *the saints* for the work of *ministry*, for building up the *body of Christ*, until we all attain to the unity of the faith and of the knowledge of the Son of God, to mature manhood, to the measure of the stature of the fullness of Christ; so that we may no longer be children, tossed to and fro and carried about with every wind of doctrine, by the cunning of men, by their craftiness in deceitful wiles. Rather, speaking the truth in love, we are to grow up in every way into him who is the head, into Christ, *from whom the whole body, joined and knit together by every joint with which it is supplied, when each part is working properly, makes bodily growth and upbuilds itself* in love. . . . assuming that you have heard about him and were taught in him, as the truth is in Jesus. Put off your old nature which belongs to your former manner of life and is corrupt through deceitful lusts, and be renewed in the spirit of your minds, and put on the new nature, created after the likeness of God in true righteousness and holiness. Therefore, put-

ting away falsehood, let everyone speak the truth with his neighbor, *for we are members one of another.*

60. Paul uses Tradition and Church motifs more often than "Scripture" and "word of God"

The words "Scripture" and "scriptures" appear fifty-one times in the New Testament. Yet in eight of his thirteen epistles (2 Corinthians, Ephesians, Philippians, Colossians, 1 and 2 Thessalonians, Titus, and Philemon) Paul never uses either of these words. In fact, Paul uses them only fourteen times altogether: in Romans (six times), 1 Corinthians (two), Galatians (three), 1 Timothy (two), and 2 Timothy (one).

In contrast, if we survey "Body" (of Christ) in Paul we find nineteen appearances: Romans 7:4; 12:4-5; 1 Corinthians 10:17; 12:12-13,25,27; Ephesians 1:23; 3:6; 4:4,12,16; 5:23,30; Colossians 1:18,24; 2:19; 3:15.

Paul uses "Church" (*ekklesia*), in more than merely a local sense of congregation or building, twenty times: 1 Corinthians 5:12; 6:4; 10:32; 11:22; 12:28; 15:9; Galatians 1:13; Ephesians 1:22; 3:10, 21; 5:23-25, 27, 29, 32; Philippians 3:6; Colossians 1:18, 24; 1 Timothy 3:15.

Likewise, in four instances Paul uses (apostolic) "tradition(s)" (*paradosis*): 1 Corinthians 11:2; Colossians 2:8; 2 Thessalonians 2:15; 3:6.

But the word "tradition" is not the only word Paul uses for this notion, not by a long shot. There is also the concept of "receiving" (tradition) and "delivering" or passing it on. Three of the above passages on "tradition" contain this motif. This mention of some sort of tradition passed down (primarily orally, through preaching) can be seen in passages such as 1 Corinthians 11:23; 15:1-2; 15:3; Galatians 1:9, 12; 1 Thessalonians 2:13; and 2 Timothy 1:13; 2:2, for eight more instances.

Moreover, there are at least fifteen other Scripture passages that exhibit the notion of apostolic (and oral) tradition, expressed in various different ways (including "word of God," "preaching," et cetera): Romans 6:17; 10:8; 16:25; 1 Corinthians 1:18; 2 Corinthians 3:6; Ephesians 1:13; Philippians 2:16; 4:9; Colossians 1:5-6; 1 Thessalonians 1:6; 2 Thessalonians 3:14; 2 Timothy 4:2, 15, 17.

Paul cites the Old Testament eighty-four times, but this does not prove or even imply *sola scriptura*—though it is consistent with the Catholic "three-legged stool" rule of faith. Paul's citations also show the importance of making a case for the gospel by appeal to Old Covenant precedent.

Protestants may want *sola scriptura* to be the Pauline rule of faith, but the numbers just don't add up.

PART TWO

The Binding Authority
of the Church

VII.
New Testament Evidence for a Hierarchical, Visible Church with Strong Authority

61. The Church can "bind and loose"

In Scripture, the Church receives from Christ a special authority: the power to bind and loose.

> Matthew 16:19: I will give you the keys of the kingdom of heaven, and whatever you bind on earth shall be bound in heaven, and whatever you loose on earth shall be loosed in heaven.

> Matthew 18:18: Whatever you bind on earth shall be bound in heaven, and whatever you loose on earth shall be loosed in heaven.

> John 20:23: If you forgive the sins of any, they are forgiven; if you retain the sins of any, they are retained.

Furthermore, St. Paul writes in 2 Corinthians 2:7, 10, "You should rather turn to forgive and comfort him . . . Any one whom you forgive, I also forgive. What I have forgiven, if I have forgiven anything, has been for your sake in the presence of Christ." These were not sins committed against Paul or the other Corinthian believers. The sinner in question appears to be the one mentioned in 1 Corinthians 5:1-5, guilty of incest.

In that passage Paul "binds" and judges the man's sins (5:3-4), and urges the Corinthians to concur in the judgment (5:4-5). When he is forgiven, it is an instance of loosing. Many Protestants will argue that only God can bind and loose with certainty. But Paul does it himself with great authority and seeming certainty! Protestants argue that priests cannot declare penalties and satisfaction, yet Paul does both. It is a sacramental, contractual exchange, involving men (priests) offering God's forgiveness for the sins of others not committed against *them*.

Binding and loosing are not already pronounced by God and only "parroted" by men; rather, they are *pronounced* by men, using their own judgment, with God's delegated authority. Such power to proclaim absolution and forgiveness to the repentant sinner goes against the notion that only Scripture itself is binding.

62. The Bible presents a universal, visible, and hierarchical Church

> Acts 15:22: Then it seemed good to the apostles and elders, with the whole church, to choose men from among them and send them to Antioch with Paul and Barnabas.

This was in the context of the Jerusalem Council. In contrast, a reference to local "churches" occurs in Acts 15:41. Another clear instance of a reference to the visible, universal Church appears in Acts 20:28:

> Take heed to yourselves and to all the flock, in which the Holy Spirit has made you overseers [*episkopoi*/bishops], to care for the church of God which he obtained with the blood of his own Son (cf. Matt. 16:18).

"Church" is singular and "bishops" are "overseers" of this biblical Church. In one verse, therefore, we observe: 1) hierarchy, 2) visibility, and 3) universality/oneness.

The Bible clearly describes a hierarchical Church government in which bishops exercise authority over priests. The (Protestant) King James translation renders *episkopos* or its cognates as "bishop" (or "bishoprick"—Acts 1:20) in 1 Timothy 3:1; 3:2; Philippians 1:1; Titus 1:7; and 1 Peter 2:25; never as "elder." The Greek word usually translated as "elder" in English Bible translations (but not as "bishop") is *presbuteros* (from which we get the word "priest") and its cognates (1 Tim. 5:1-2, 17, 19; Titus 1:5; James 5:14; 1 Pet. 5:1,5; eighteen times in the book of Acts).

There is such a thing in the Bible as a bishop who oversees the *presbuteros* ("priest" or "minister"). Bishops are described as having the following responsibilities, above and beyond those of the ordinary priest:

A) Jurisdiction over local churches and priests, and the power to bestow ordination (Acts 14:22; 1 Tim. 5:22; 2 Tim. 1:6; Titus 1:5).

B) Particular duty to defend the faith (apologetics) (Acts 20:28-31; 2 Tim. 4:1-5; Titus 1:9-10; 2 Pet. 3:15-16).

C) Rebuking of false doctrine and to confer excommunication (Acts 8:14-24; 1 Cor. 16:22; 1 Tim. 5:20; 2 Tim. 4:2; Titus 1:10-11).

D) Presiding over confirmation (receiving the Holy Spirit in greater measure) (Acts 8:14-17; 19:5-6).

E) Management of church finances (1 Tim. 3:3-4; 1 Pet. 5:2).

Still, *"sola ecclesia"* would be an inaccurate description of the Catholic system of authority. This is not a Catholic term (unlike *sola scriptura*, which is the Protestant's own term). When it comes to earthly authority to preserve and teach revealed truths, we don't believe in "Church alone." We believe in the "three-legged stool" of Bible, Church, and Tradition, which is quite a different concept indeed. The implicit (dichotomous) reasoning here seems to be: "If you don't accept Bible alone, you must believe in Church alone," as if there were no other possible positions besides the choice of one extreme or another.

63. *Anathema* and excommunication are biblical concepts

The vivid Greek term *anathema*, meaning "accursed," is directed by Church councils primarily at doctrines rather than persons. It is based on the ancient practice in the Church of condemning heretical teachings—a procedure derived biblically from passages such as Galatians 1:8-9 and 1 Corinthians 16:22 (the latter has *anathema* both in Greek and in many English versions). It is a proper function of the Church to define correct doctrine and to reject contrary notions—Paul does this constantly—not to define people's eternal destiny.

Most emphatically, then: neither *anathema* nor *excommunication* means "proclaimed *damned* (by the Church)," as many Protestants mistakenly suppose. Rather, it means being "out of the Church" (because of divergence from its doctrines) or "out of communion" (with the sacraments and the Christian fellowship of believers).

Excommunication is perfectly in accord with Pauline practices and teachings as expounded in, for example, 1 Corinthians 5:3-5; 2 Thessalonians 3:6; 1 Timothy 1:19-20; 2 Timothy 2:14-19; 4:14-15, as well as with our Lord's express injunction in Matthew 18:15-18. Peter also utters an anathema against Ananias and Sapphira, one that was emphatically affirmed by God (Acts 5:2-11).

Again, we see that such strong, binding, unquestioned central human authority in the Church signifies an infallible Church, in which case, it is untrue that Scripture is the only infallible authority.

64. Scripture has problematic areas to work through, too

Protestants like to point to scandalous moments in Church history as disproofs of Church authority. It is true, there are "problems" in Catholic history to mull over and attempt to resolve (for example, popes and antipopes simultaneously claiming the Chair of Peter). Likewise, there are exegetical "problems" in Scripture, which Protestants devote much energy to resolving. (I have Gleason Archer's *Encyclopedia of Bible Difficulties* in my library.) As the latter are not regarded as antithetical to belief in an inspired, inerrant, and infallible Bible, difficulties in Church history are not fatal to belief in an infallible Church.

65. Jesus' mention of "sheep and shepherd" does not imply an invisible Church

Some Protestants contend that Jesus himself suggested that the Church was first and foremost "invisible," not bound by denominational structures. They cite his analogy of the sheep and the shepherd (John 10:1-16; cf. 2 Tim. 2:19; 1 John 2:19) who know each other to show that the Church is a mystical, invisible body consisting of the elect and truly saved only.

But Scripture also describes the *unsaved reprobate* as "sheep" (Ps. 74:1), refers to "sheep" that have "gone astray" (Ps. 119:176), and applies the description to the nation of Israel (Ezek. 34:2-3, 13, 23, 30), and indeed, all men (Isa. 53:6). The overall biblical theme concerning "sheep" is in the sense that all men, and particularly Israel, are his children. This doesn't require an invisible Church or forbid a visible, institutional Church, because the latter is clearly indicated in the Bible.

66. Authority has to have "teeth"

Protestants want to retain the "authority" (in some sense) of a "teaching church." But Catholics wonder: Of what use is "authority" if it is not binding? One could contend that this is foreign to the very meaning of the word. Police have authority because they can compel action and arrest people against their will. The IRS has authority because it can collect income tax and punish those who do not comply. Judges have authority because they can compel and sentence. Teachers have authority over students; so do school principals, who can expel students; and so forth. Although "authority" isn't strictly synonymous with "having the power to compel," practically speaking they go hand-in-hand.

But then we get to Protestant human "authority," which in the end is really no authority at all, because Luther said "here *I* stand," appealing to the abstract notion of "evident reasoning" and to "clear Scripture." The *individual* decides; the "authority" has only an advisory capacity. One may have immense respect for an advisor, but he is still only that. A presidential advisor, for instance, can always be overruled by the president. He gives advice, but he has no power to compel.

It is clear in the Bible that apostolic, ecclesiastical authority is binding and unquestionable. St. Paul always assumes that he has authority over the churches he is writing to. The bishops also have strong authority, as seen in preceding sections. The Jerusalem Council (Acts 15) had such authority that it equated its opinions with those of God the Holy Spirit (15:28), and Paul "delivered" the "decisions" of the Council for "observance" (Acts 16:4). There is not the slightest hint, here or anywhere else, that Church authority or apostolic tradition was to be questioned at all, let alone revolted against wholesale as happened in the Protestant revolt in the sixteenth century.

67. According to Scripture, the bishop's role is distinct and important

Protestants will concede that the word "bishop" appears in the Bible but deny that hierarchical distinctions are implied. Moreover, they will argue that in the Bible bishops, elders, and deacons are synonymous terms for the same office—roughly that of a modern pastor—and that it doesn't indicate that bishops are above these other offices. In Titus 1:5, however, the bishop is higher than an elder because he is charged to "appoint" them "in every town." This suggests both hierarchy and regional administration or jurisdiction.

Both bishops and deacons are mentioned in Philippians 1:1, which would be odd if they were synonymous. 1 Timothy 3:1-7 also discusses bishops, then goes on to treat deacons separately in 3:8-10 ("Deacons likewise..."). We would expect some overlapping or variability in function of ministers in the early Church, because it was just the beginning of the development of ecclesiology.

The doctrine of the Church and its government took time to develop, just as the Trinitarian and Christological doctrine would develop over several centuries. Even Paul called himself a "minister" or deacon (Greek: *diakonos*) more than once (1 Cor. 3:5; 2 Cor. 3:6; 6:4; Eph. 3:7; Col. 1:23, 25), but no one thinks that is *all* he was.

VIII.
Biblical Indications of Apostolic Succession

68. Paul passed on his office to Timothy

If St. Paul passes on his own office, and he is an apostle, this is harmonious with the notion of apostolic succession. His own words certainly imply such a succession:

1 Timothy 6:20: O Timothy, guard what has been entrusted to you.

2 Timothy 1:6: Hence I remind you to rekindle the gift of God that is within you through the laying on of my hands.

2 Timothy 1:13-14: Follow the pattern of the sound words which you have heard from me, in the faith and love which are in Christ Jesus; guard the truth that has been entrusted to you by the Holy Spirit who dwells within us.

2 Timothy 2:1-2: You then, my son, be strong in the grace that is in Christ Jesus, and what you have heard from me before many witnesses entrust to faithful men who will be able to teach others also.

69. The Bible explicitly demonstrates apostolic succession

Paul teaches us in Ephesians 2:20 that the Church is built on the foundation of the apostles, whom Christ himself chose (John 6:70; Acts 1:2, 13; cf. Matt. 16:18). In Mark 6:30 the twelve original disciples of Jesus are called apostles, and Matthew 10:1-5 and Revelation 21:14 speak of the twelve apostles. After Judas defected, the remaining eleven apostles appointed his successor, Matthias (Acts 1:20-26). Since Judas is called a bishop (*episkopee*) in this passage (1:20), then by logical extension all the apostles can be considered bishops (albeit of an extraordinary sort).

If the apostles are bishops, and one of them is replaced by another after the death, resurrection, and ascension of Christ, then we have an explicit example of *apostolic succession* in the Bible. This succession shows an authoritative equivalency between apostles and bishops, who are the successors of the apostles. As a corollary, we are also informed in Scripture that the Church itself is perpetual, infallible, and indefectible (Matt. 16:18; John 14:26; 16:18).

70. Neither Scripture nor the Church Fathers rule out Tradition or apostolic succession

On what basis do Protestants conclude that "word of mouth" (tradition) was reliable only for a hundred years or so? We agree when they say that the *apostolic age* ceased around A.D. 100. (We also agree that public revelation ceased around the same time.) But why would they make the leap that all non-apostolic tradition was *unreliable*? Where does that come from? The Bible itself doesn't state such a thing.

The Church Fathers seemed to show no awareness of this alleged sea change in authority. St. Ignatius of Antioch gives extraordinary authority to the bishops. St. Clement of Rome functions as a strong bishop (if not a pope) in his letters. Other early Fathers (particularly St. Irenaeus, but many others) explicitly teach apostolic succession and appeal to it as an unimpeachable authority, along with scriptural proofs, in combating the heretics.

71. The Catholic "epistemology of authority" is a combination of faith, history, and reason

Jesus is the incarnate God. He performed miracles. He rose from the dead, and proved it by "many infallible proofs" (Acts

1:3). There was one recognized deposit of faith (Acts 2:42; Jude 3). Jesus established a Church, with Peter as its head (Matt. 16:13-20). This Church has certain characteristics, described in the Bible. Apostolic succession was the criterion of orthodoxy for the Fathers. The Catholic Church traces itself back via this unbroken line, centered in Rome and on the papacy.

A Catholic accepts all this in faith; but it is based on reasonable consideration of the historical criteria, just as one would accept the historicity of the Resurrection or the authority of the Bible. Since the deposit of faith was one unified teaching, there necessarily had to be one Church that preserved it and promulgated it.

God has the power to preserve apostolic doctrine inviolate and to protect the true Church from error. It requires *faith* to believe this, and that is what a Catholic does: We have faith that this Church can exist and that it can be identified and located. We don't say this rests on our own individual choice. It is already there; it is like our "stumbling upon" the Pacific Ocean or Mount Everest—we don't determine whether the thing exists or not. And we must believe by faith it is what it claims to be.

Why should that surprise anyone except a person who thinks that Christianity is determined by arbitrary choice and rationalism without faith? The Christian faith is not simply philosophy or subjective preference, as if Christianity were reduced to Philosophy 101 (where someone might prefer Kierkegaard to Kant) or the selection of a flavor of ice cream. If we are to be biblical, the Bible refers often to a "passed-down tradition." It is out there. It exists.

It is not necessary for each Catholic to have infallible certainty (as some Protestant critics argue is an inherent fault in our system); they simply have to accept the teaching, most conveniently presented in the *Catechism of the Catholic Church*. To assert that every Catholic must have personal infallible certainty of infallible doctrines, one must presuppose that every

Christian believer is a philosopher, with a special grasp of epistemology—a patently ridiculous notion.

IX.
The Jerusalem Council and Its Implications for Subsequent Catholic Ecclesiology

72. Participants at the Jerusalem Council, guided by the Holy Spirit, asserted a binding authority

If the Holy Spirit could speak to a council in apostolic times, he can do so now. Why would that state of affairs change? This doesn't require belief in ongoing revelation, which is another issue. Our Lord Jesus told the disciples at the Last Supper that the Holy Spirit would "teach you all things" (John 14:26) and "guide you into all truth" (John 16:13). This can be understood either as referring to individuals alone, or in a corporate sense, or both. If it is corporate, then it could apply to a Church council. And in fact, we see exactly that in the Jerusalem Council in Acts 15:1-29.

Its authority was binding because it was a council of the Church, guided by the Holy Spirit (as Scripture expressly tells us: Acts 15:6, 22, 28). It would have been binding on Christians if there had never been a New Testament (and at that time there wasn't one), or if it had never been recorded in Scripture.

The Jerusalem Council actively exercised its authority to compel. It issued *commands*, not scholarly opinions from an ivory tower. Paul and his assistants Silas and Timothy proclaimed these decisions in their missionary travels:

> Acts 16:4-5: As they went on their way through the cities, they delivered to them for observance the decisions which had been reached by the apostles and elders who were at Jerusalem. So the churches were strengthened in the faith, and they increased in numbers daily.

The Jerusalem Council is a crystal-clear scriptural example of infallible Church authority. In Acts, the early Church's government is shown to be of a certain nature, and the Jerusalem Council is described as having arrived at an infallible decision. It makes sense to say that the nature of Church government endured, and that subsequent Church councils throughout history also arrived at infallible decisions.

73. The Jerusalem Council made binding decisions with no great reliance on Scripture

In a doctrinal dispute recorded in Scripture we find assembled bishops (James is generally considered by historians to have been the bishop of Jerusalem) and "apostles and elders" in Jerusalem, in council (Acts 15:6), settling disputes without mentioning Scripture. It is true that James does quote the Old Testament concerning the Gentiles' coming into the fold of God's people (15:16-18); but the main decision of the council (often called an "apostolic decree") was given without any biblical rationale whatsoever:

> Acts 15:29: It has seemed good to the Holy Spirit and to us to lay upon you no greater burden than these necessary things: that you abstain from what has been sacrificed to idols and from blood and from what is strangled and from unchastity. (cf. 15:20)

There are plenty of passages about circumcision in the Old Testament, but none of them were mentioned (at least not in the record we have of the proceedings). Prior to the decision, Peter also spoke about the Gentiles, but apparently gave no scriptural support (15:7-11). Evidently, then, this authoritative council (including Paul, Peter, and James) was what many Protestants would call "unbiblical." When the time came to make its decision, the Bible wasn't mentioned (this was also often true in later ecumenical councils, such as those held at Nicaea and Chalcedon). If *sola scriptura* were true, this could never happen.

74. Paul's apostolic calling was subordinated to Peter's authority and the larger Church

Paul's ministry was not "self-validating." After his conversion, he went to Jerusalem specifically to see Peter (Gal. 1:18). He was initially commissioned by Peter, James, and John (Gal. 2:9) to preach to the Gentiles. In Acts 15:2-3 we are told that "Paul and Barnabas and some of the others were appointed to go up to Jerusalem to the apostles and the elders about this question. So, being sent their way by the church," they went off on their assignment.

That is hardly consistent with the idea of Paul being the "pope" or leading figure in the hierarchy of authority; he was directed by others, as one under orders. When we see Paul and Peter together in the Council of Jerusalem (Acts 15:6-29), we observe that Peter wields an authority that Paul doesn't possess.

We learn that "after there was much debate, Peter rose" to address the assembly (15:7). The Bible records his speech, which goes on for five verses. Then it reports that "all the assembly kept silence" (15:12). Paul and Barnabas speak next, not making authoritative pronouncements, but confirming Peter's exposition, speaking about "signs and wonders God had done through them among the Gentiles" (15:12). Then, when James speaks, he refers right back to what "Simeon [Peter] has related" (15:14). Why did James skip right over Paul's comments and go back to what Peter said? Paul and his associates are subsequently "sent off" by the Council, and they "delivered the letter" (15:30; cf. 16:4).

None of this seems consistent with the notion that Paul was above, or even equal to, Peter in authority. But it's perfectly consistent with Peter's having a preeminent authority. Paul was under the authority of the council, and Peter (along with James, as the Bishop of Jerusalem) presided over it. Paul and Barnabas were sent by "the church" (of Antioch: see 14:26). Then, they were sent by the Jerusalem Council (15:25, 30), which was guided by the Holy Spirit (15:28), back to Antioch (15:30).

X.
Biblical Analogies for an Infallible Church

75. Old Testament Levites were granted the gift of special protection from error

> Malachi 2:6-7: True instruction was in his mouth, and no wrong was found on his lips. He walked with me in peace and uprightness, and he turned many from iniquity. For the lips of a priest should guard knowledge, and men should seek instruction from his mouth, for he is the messenger of the LORD of hosts.

Biblical passages such as this one and those in the next two sections are offered (I reiterate) as *analogies*, not proofs. This particular statement is a rather good analogy for the purpose, especially the words "true instruction . . . no wrong was found on his lips," which are *precisely* what constitutes infallibility (literally, the inability to fail or falter). The person so described gives instruction and is a messenger from God, analogous to (as a sort of "type and shadow" of) an infallible Church. The Church has greater gifts and protections than the Old Testament "Church" had, but there were significant and striking precursors in many respects already present in Old Testament times.

76. Prophets exercised binding teaching authority and possessed virtual infallibility

The assumed infallibility of prophets and other authority figures in the Old Testament is virtually identical, by analogy, to popes, councils, and bishops in the Catholic Church. Popes are believed to be infallible, as are councils in agreement with the pope (under carefully specified conditions). Ancient Judaism lacked one absolute figure like the pope, but when one was in the presence of an Ezra or Jeremiah or Samuel, it made little practical difference.

John the Baptist was considered the last of the prophets (cf. Malachi 4:5 and Matthew 11:14; 17:12; Mark 9:13; Luke 1:17). Yet Jesus said of him, "I tell you, among those born of women none is greater than John; yet he who is least in the kingdom of God is greater than he" (Luke 7:28; cf. Matt. 11:11). How much more, then, should we expect infallibility to be in place in the far greater New Covenant? Here are some of the many relevant passages along these lines:

> Numbers 12:6: And he said, "Hear my words: If there is a prophet among you, I the LORD make myself known to him in a vision, I speak with him in a dream."

> Deuteronomy 18:18: I will raise up for them a prophet like you from among their brethren; and I will put my words in his mouth, and he shall speak to them all that I command him.

> 2 Kings 17:13: Yet the LORD warned Israel and Judah by every prophet and every seer, saying, "Turn from your evil ways and keep my commandments and my statutes, in accordance with all the law which I commanded your fathers, and which I sent to you by my servants the prophets."

> 2 Kings 21:10: And the LORD said by his servants the prophets.

> 2 Chronicles 29:25: . . . for the commandment was from the LORD through his prophets.

> Jeremiah 35:15: I have sent to you all my servants the prophets

> Jeremiah 42:4: Jeremiah the prophet said to them, "I have heard you; behold, I will pray to the LORD your God according to your request, and whatever the LORD answers you I will tell you; I will keep nothing back from you."

Daniel 9:6: We have not listened to thy servants the prophets, who spoke in thy name.

Daniel 9:10: . . . and have not obeyed the voice of the LORD our God by following his laws, which he set before us by his servants the prophets.

Amos 3:7: Surely the Lord GOD does nothing, without revealing his secret to his servants the prophets.

Zechariah 7:12: They made their hearts like adamant lest they should hear the law and the words which the LORD of hosts had sent by his Spirit through the former prophets.

77. Prophets proclaimed the inspired "word of the Lord"

To purport to speak the "word of the Lord" is a far grander claim than papal infallibility, which is a negative protection against error, not direct on-the-spot inspiration. Yet that is precisely what Scripture tells us the prophets did.

1 Samuel 15:10: The word of the Lord came to Samuel.

2 Samuel 23:2: The Spirit of the LORD speaks by me, his word is upon my tongue. [King David]

1 Chronicles 17:3: But that same night the word of the LORD came to Nathan.

Isaiah 38:4: Then the word of the LORD came to Isaiah.

Jeremiah 26:15: The LORD sent me to you to speak all these words in your ears.

Ezekiel 33:1: The word of the LORD came to me.

Haggai 1:13: Then Haggai, the messenger of the LORD, spoke to the people with the LORD's message, "I am with you, says the LORD."

The prophets received their inspiration from the Holy Spirit (2 Chron. 24:20; Neh. 9:30; Zech. 7:12). Jesus assured the disciples that the same Holy Spirit would guide them "into all the truth" (John 16:13; cf. 8:32) to help them carry out their duties as shepherds and teachers of the Christian flock.

78. God uses fallible men to perform infallible works

Protestants believe that God could produce an infallible Bible by means of fallible, sinful men (such as Moses, David, Matthew, Peter, and Paul), that it could be confirmed in its parameters by fallible, sinful men, translated by fallible, sinful men, and preserved for 1,500 years before Protestantism by fallible, sinful men. We agree, and contend that God can and does, likewise, create and sustain the infallible Church and Tradition to which this same Bible repeatedly refers. This is not a whit less credible or plausible, and indeed is required by the same Bible.

79. God is able to preserve both Bible and Church from error

Protestants usually contend either that God is unable to preserve Christian doctrine without error by means of an imperfect Church run by fallen, fallible men; or, that he is able to do so but chose not to.

James R. White illustrates the first viewpoint:

It is simply impossible to have two ultimate sources of authority. One will either subjugate tradition to Scripture (as the Reformers taught) or one will subjugate Scripture to tradition, and this is what we see in Roman Catholicism. The Pharisees, too, denied that they were in any way denigrating the authority of Scripture by their adherence to the "traditions of their fathers." But Jesus did not accept their claim. He knew better. He pointed out how their traditions destroyed the very purpose of God's law, allowing them to circumvent the clear teachings of the Word through the agency of their traditions. . . . If Christ was right to condemn the Pharisees for their false traditions, then the traditions of Rome, too, must be condemned.[12]

William Whitaker, in his renowned work, *A Disputation on Holy Scripture,* provides an example of the latter point of view:

I confess that the divine Providence can preserve from destruction whatever it chooses; for God can do whatever he wills. But if we choose thus to abuse the divine Providence, we may, in the same manner, infer that there is no need of the scriptures, that every thing should be trusted to the Divine Providence, and nothing committed to writing, because God can preserve religion safe without the scriptures. But God hath nowhere promised that he will save and protect unwritten traditions from being lost: consequently, the church and tradition are not parallel cases. I can produce innumerable testimonies and promises wherewith God hath bound himself to the church to preserve it: let them produce any such promises of God respecting the preservation of traditions. Now this they cannot do. Secondly, I confess that God preserved his doctrine from Adam to Moses orally transmitted, that is, in the form of unwritten tradition. It cannot be denied. But then it was amongst exceeding few persons: for the great majority had corrupted this doctrine.[13]

How could a Protestant assert scenario A? It seems to deny God's omnipotence. Why do those who hold to scenario B think God would not protect true theology from corruption, especially in light of the biblical teaching that the Holy Spirit will guide us into all truth (John 14:26; 15:26; 16:13)? It makes no sense to believe that, if there is a Church at all, God would not protect it from error. If the Holy Spirit guides us into the truth, then we will "be one" as Christians, "even as" the Father, Son, and Holy Spirit are one (John 17:11). The Protestant's skeptical view of Church infallibility implies that God is either unable to preserve his truth or unwilling to. Neither scenario sounds like the God we know, as revealed in Scripture.

If Protestants want to shoot down all infallibility as an illegitimate philosophical concept or basis of certainty (real or imagined), and to adopt the course of epistemological skepticism, they are free to do so. But most of them (at least the Evangelicals and other more-traditional Protestants) do proclaim and believe in the infallibility (and inerrancy) of Scripture, which leads them to the problem of the canon: before we can believe in an infallible Scripture, someone or something has to tell us, infallibly, what Scripture is.

It should be noted that Protestants use the word *infallibility* in a broader fashion than Catholics do. We prefer the word *inerrant* (without error) in reference to Scripture, and usually apply *infallibility* (literally, inability to fail) only to councils and popes or to the Church, whereas Protestants apply both terms to Scripture, meaning not only that it is without error, but also that it is unable to fail in its purpose. Accordingly, James White illustrates how Protestants use the word *infallibility* when referring to the Bible:

> The Scriptures are, as God-breathed revelation, sufficient to provide the "rule of faith" necessary for the Church's mission in this world. Further, the Scriptures provide an *infallible* rule of faith, one that cannot err . . . the Scriptures themselves do not change and therefore provide the Church with a firm foundation.[14]

80. Messy deliberations and other difficulties do not disprove the infallibility of councils

The deliberations that take place in Church councils can be messy. There will be disagreement and expressions of erroneous positions. Despite the problem of their own doctrinal chaos (or perhaps in order to feel better about it), Protestants sometimes point to such contentious council deliberations as proof that councils are not infallible.

But Catholics believe that the Holy Spirit protects the results of a council from error, not that he inspires every word in its process. Indeed, that councils have produced orthodox declarations of doctrine (much of which even Protestants agree with) despite the errors and disagreements that surfaced during their deliberations, *suggests*, rather than disproves, God's protective hand.

Likewise, difficulties in application of council decisions, or decisions that not all understand with immediate clarity, do not disprove councils' authority. On this point I always quote C. S. Lewis who said, "the rules of chess create chess problems." Yes, there are "problems" to work through in a chess game, but they don't cast into doubt the rules themselves—just as the textual questions and other Bible difficulties that nonbelievers cite (and which Protestants themselves love to discuss and debate) do not undermine Scripture's inerrancy.

81. Biblical truth and Tradition are much larger than just the gospel message

As the doctrinal disunity in Protestantism reveals, an invisible, non-institutional Church can't really be the "pillar and bulwark of the truth" as the Bible says it is (1 Tim. 3:15). Some Protestants try to argue around this by asserting that "truth" in this passage refers to the gospel only—defining "gospel" along the lines of "justification by faith alone in the finished work of Christ on the cross." (A better biblical definition would be the incarnation, life, death, resurrection, and ascension of Christ (Acts 2:22-40; 13:16-41; 1 Cor. 15:1-8).

This narrow definition of "truth" is not at all obvious, and nothing in the immediate context supports it. We know that the gospel is not the sum and total of Christian truth, as evidenced in the many instances of "truth" (Gk., *aletheia* and cognates) in the New Testament. For example, John 16:13: "When the Spirit of truth comes, he will guide you into all the truth." Jesus was speaking to the disciples, who were obviously already believers who had received, understood, and accepted the gospel.

Therefore, the "truth" referred to must include more than the gospel itself. In fact, the later part of the same verse proves this: "he will declare to you the things that are to come." In Romans 1:18 Paul refers to wicked men who "suppress the truth." This truth, in context, goes beyond the gospel to "what can be known about God" (1:19): his "eternal power and deity." God's attributes are not the gospel (cf. 1:25: "the truth about God").

The larger meaning in many places can be seen in any linguistic reference work, such as Vine's *Expository Dictionary*, Kittel, Robertson, Vincent, Thayer, or other such aids. Jesus says "I am the truth" (John 14:6). Obviously, he didn't mean, "I am the gospel." Granted, "church" has a wide latitude of meaning in the New Testament. Whether it means "all believers" in 1 Timothy 3:15, or a more strict meaning of an organization with bishops, et cetera (or both) may be disputed by well-meaning exegetes in good faith.

82. 1 Timothy 3:15 proves the infallibility of the Catholic Church

> 1 Timothy 3:15: If I am delayed, you may know how one ought to behave in the household of God, which is the church of the living God, the pillar and bulwark of the truth.

Pillars and foundations support things and prevent them from collapsing. To be a "bulwark" of the truth means to be a "safety net" against truth turning into falsity. If the Church could err, it could not be what Scripture says it is. God's truth would be the house built on a foundation of sand in Jesus' parable. For this passage of Scripture to be true, the Church could not err—it must be infallible. A similar passage may cast further light on 1 Timothy 3:15:

> Ephesians 2:19-21: You are fellow citizens with the saints and members of the household of God, built upon the foundation of the apostles and prophets, Christ Jesus himself being the cornerstone, in whom the whole structure is joined together and grows into a holy temple in the Lord.

1 Timothy 3:15 defines "household of God" as "the church of the living God." Therefore, we know that Ephesians 2:19-21 is also referring to the Church, even though that word is not present. Here, the Church's own "foundation" is "the apostles and prophets, Christ Jesus himself being the cornerstone." The foundation of the Church itself is Jesus and apostles and prophets.

Prophets spoke "in the name of the Lord" (1 Chron. 21:19; 2 Chron. 33:18; Jer. 26:9), and commonly introduced their utterances with "thus says the Lord" (Isa. 10:24; Jer. 4:3; 26:4; Ezek. 13:8; Amos 3:11-12; and many more). They spoke the "word of the Lord" (Isa. 1:10; 38:4; Jer. 1:2; 13:3, 8; 14:1; Ezek. 13:1-2; Hos. 1:1; Joel 1:1; Jon. 1:1; Mic. 1:1, et cetera). These communications cannot contain any untruths insofar as they truly originate from God, with the prophet serving as a spokesman or intermediary of God (Jer. 2:2; 26:8; Ezek. 11:5; Zech. 1:6; and many more). Likewise, apostles proclaimed truth unmixed with error (1 Cor. 2:7-13; 1 Tim. 2:7; 2 Tim. 1:11-14; 2 Pet. 1:12-21).

Does this foundation have any faults or cracks? Since Jesus is the cornerstone, he can hardly be a faulty foundation. Neither can the apostles or prophets err when teaching the inspired gospel message or proclaiming God's word. In the way that apostles and prophets are infallible, so is the Church set up by our Lord

Jesus Christ. We ourselves (all Christians) are incorporated into the Church (following the metaphor), on top of the foundation.

> 1 Peter 2:4-9: Come to him, to that living stone, rejected by men but in God's sight chosen and precious, and like living stones be yourselves built into a spiritual house, to be a holy priesthood, to offer spiritual sacrifices acceptable to God through Jesus Christ. For it stands in scripture: "Behold, I am laying in Zion a stone, a cornerstone chosen and precious, and he who believes in him will not be put to shame." To you therefore who believe, he is precious, but for those who do not believe, "The very stone which the builders rejected has become the head of the corner," and "A stone that will make men stumble, a rock that will make them fall"; for they stumble because they disobey the word, as they were destined to do. But you are a chosen race, a royal priesthood, a holy nation, God's own people, that you may declare the wonderful deeds of him who called you out of darkness into his marvelous light (cf. Isa. 28:16).

Jesus is without fault or untruth, and he is the cornerstone of the Church. The Church is also more than once even *identified with Jesus himself* by being called his "Body" (Acts 9:5 cf. with 22:4 and 26:11; 1 Cor. 12:27; Eph. 1:22-23; 4:12; 5:23, 30; Col. 1:24). That the Church is so intimately connected with Jesus, who is infallible, is itself a strong argument that the Church is also infallible and without error.

Therefore, the Church is built on the foundation of Jesus (perfect in all knowledge) and the prophets and apostles (who spoke infallible truth, often recorded in inspired, inerrant Scripture). Moreover, it is the very "body of Christ." It stands to reason that the Church itself is infallible, by the same token. In the Bible, nowhere is truth presented as anything less than *pure* truth, unmixed with error. That was certainly how Paul conceived his own "tradition" that he received and passed down.

Knowing what truth is, how can its own foundation or pillar be something *less* than total truth (since truth itself contains no falsehoods, untruths, lies, or errors)? It cannot. It is impossible. It is a straightforward matter of logic and plain observation. A stream cannot rise above its source. What is built upon a foundation cannot be *greater* than the foundation. If it were, the whole structure would collapse.

If an elephant stood on the shoulders of a man as its foundation, that foundation would collapse. The base of a skyscraper has to hold the weight above it. The foundations of a suspension bridge over a river have to be strong enough to support that bridge.

Therefore, we must conclude that if the Church is the *foundation* of truth, then the Church *must* be *infallible*, since truth is infallible, and the foundation cannot be lesser than that which is built upon it. And since there is another infallible authority apart from Scripture, *sola scriptura* must be false.

83. The Church is indefectible, because Jesus is its foundation and because God dwells in his "temple"[15]

1 Corinthians 3:9, 11, 16: For we are God's fellow workers; you are God's field, God's building. . . . For no other foundation can anyone lay than that which is laid, which is Jesus Christ. . . . Do you not know that you are God's temple and that God's Spirit dwells in you?

1 Corinthians 6:19: Do you not know that your body is a temple of the Holy Spirit within you, which you have from God? You are not your own.

Ephesians 3:20-21: Now to him who by the power at work within us is able to do far more abundantly than all that we ask or think, to him be glory in the church and in Christ Jesus to all generations, forever and ever. Amen.

Colossians 1:17-18: He is before all things, and in him all things hold together. He is the head of the body, the church; he is the beginning, the first-born from the dead, that in everything he might be pre-eminent.

XI.
The Biblical Prohibition of Denominationalism, Theological Relativism, and Indifferentism

84. Protestant sectarianism contradicts biblical requirements of doctrinal agreement

God and the biblical writers always intended "one faith, one baptism" (Eph. 4:5). Having even *two* contradictory beliefs on revealed Christian truths is already scandalous and unbiblical. Only one received doctrine, or "deposit of faith" exists—not two, not five, not fifteen, nor hundreds. The error starts beyond one.

In John 17:22 Jesus prays that the disciples would be "one, as we are one." He is referring to the oneness of the Father and the Son. And in John 17:23, he desires that they (and we) be "perfectly one." It is pretty difficult to maintain that this does not include perfect doctrinal agreement.

The Father and the Son do not differ on how one is saved, on the true nature of the Eucharist and the sacraments, on the authority of the Bible and the Church. So how can Protestants, who differ greatly on such things, possibly claim the "perfect oneness" that mirrors that of the Persons of the Godhead?

St. Paul testifies to the importance of doctrinal oneness by always presupposing one doctrine and one Church that preserves it:

Galatians 1:23: He . . . is now preaching the faith he once tried to destroy.

1 Timothy 1:2: To Timothy, my true child in the faith.

1 Timothy 3:9: They must hold the mystery of the faith with a clear conscience.

1 Timothy 4:1: Some will depart from the faith by giving heed to deceitful spirits and doctrines of demons.

1 Timothy 4:6: Nourished on the words of the faith and of the good doctrine which you have followed.

Titus 1:4: To Titus, my true child in a common faith (cf. Acts 6:7; Jude 3).

Paul commands, "take note of those who create dissensions and difficulties, in opposition to the doctrine which you have been taught; avoid them" (Rom. 16:17). In 1 Corinthians 1:10, he desires that there be "no dissensions," and that Christians be "united in the same mind and the same judgment." He goes on to condemn "quarreling" in 1:11, and asks in 1:13, "Is Christ divided?" In 1 Corinthians 3:3, Paul says that whatever group has "jealousy and strife" are "of the flesh" (rather than of the spirit as they should be). In 1 Corinthians 11:18-19 he seems to equate "divisions" and "factions," and he calls for "no discord" in 1 Corinthians 12:25 (cf. Rom. 13:13; 2 Cor. 12:20; Phil. 2:2; Titus 3:9; James 3:16, 1 Tim. 6:3-5; 2 Pet. 2:1). What additional evidence is needed to show that denominationalism is a sin and hence not God's will?

In fact, nothing is more strongly and repeatedly condemned in the Bible than divisions, sectarianism, and denominationalism. Our Lord Jesus viewed the Church as being "one flock" with "one shepherd" (John 10:16). St. Luke described the earliest Christians as being "of one heart and soul" (Acts 4:32). St. Peter warned about "false teachers" among Christians, who would "secretly bring in destructive heresies," which go against "the way of truth" (2 Pet. 2:1-2). Paul, above all, repeatedly condemns "enmity" and "party spirit" (Gal. 5:20), and calls for Christians to be "of the same mind, having the same love, being in full accord and of one mind" (Phil. 2:2). He condemns party affiliations associated with persons (1 Cor. 3:4-7). Paul's strong teaching on this topic is well summed up in the following two passages.

1 Timothy 6:3-5: If any one teaches otherwise and does not agree with the sound words of our Lord Jesus Christ and

the teaching which accords with godliness, he is puffed up with conceit, he knows nothing; he has a morbid craving for controversy and for disputes about words, which produce envy, dissension, slander, base suspicions, and wrangling among men who are depraved in mind and bereft of the truth, imagining that godliness is a means of gain.

Titus 3:9-11: But avoid stupid controversies, genealogies, dissensions, and quarrels over the law, for they are unprofitable and futile. As for a man who is factious, after admonishing him once or twice, have nothing more to do with him, knowing that such a person is perverted and sinful; he is self-condemned.

85. Protestantism's resignation to uncertainty leads to theological relativism

The first Protestants believed strongly enough in each of their sects to anathematize the "dissidents" outside of them. But over time, Protestantism's inability to achieve doctrinal unity led people to view disputed doctrines as unimportant, reducing the "essence" of Christianity to an ever-smaller set of doctrines. The result was an ever more liberal and relativistic view of Christianity. The theological modernism that arose after the Enlightenment flourishes to this day.

Many Protestants, whether theologically conservative or liberal, look down their noses at those who have strong convictions about "non-essentials" and consider themselves above the battles of centuries past. Others abhor the reductionist approach of modernism and maintain a belief in orthodoxy on matters great and small (even if they can't truly justify why their version of orthodoxy is more authoritative than that of another Protestant tradition). Many of them can see how compromising on some doctrines leads to a lack of faith in even the "essential" ones, as the rampant indifferentism of modern mainstream Protestantism attests. Yet, they don't seem to realize that the sin of denominationalism, which arises when men reject the authority of the Church in favor of their own interpretations, inevitably leads to liberalism.

Catholics believe that God cares enough about doctrinal truth to guarantee its continued existence through history. God never intended for us to spend our whole lives *searching* for the truth. He wants us to receive it in faith, passed down from the apostles and preserved in the Catholic Church, and to *live* it.

Protestants too often seem to equate Christianity and Christian revelation with mere philosophy or science or the arts, which is a thoroughly secular epistemology, especially when they imply that no more certainty can be achieved in Christianity, than, say, in biology or astronomy or algebra. That is preposterous. God (speaking through Paul) condemns those who are "always being instructed and can never arrive at knowledge of the truth" (2 Tim. 3:7).

It is almost as if there is a "cult of uncertainty" today in some Protestant circles. It is fashionable and tolerant (and all the other buzzwords) to be uncertain, so that one is not perceived as "triumphalistic," closed-minded," "rigid," or "fundamentalist."

Some Protestants argue that it is, in fact, God's will that we accept "diversity" within the biblical framework, pointing to Deuteronomy 29:29 and its mention of the unrevealed "secret things" that "belong to the LORD our God". But as we have seen, it is impossible to reconcile with the Scripture that repeatedly urges unity in one faith, the idea that God would permit contradiction, and thus error, in articles of faith. As for Deuteronomy 29:29, the context of the entire chapter suggests strongly that "secret things" is a reference to God's providence and foreknowledge and sovereignty—the ways in which he is far higher than us. The verse goes on to say that "the revealed things belong to us and to our children forever, to observe all the words of this law." Revelation is placed outside the realm of "secret things"—because it *belongs to us*.

Not only does Scripture teach that there is one truth, one tradition, one faith, one teaching, but, in contrast to the uncertainty and even despair that *sola scriptura* produces, Jesus and the Bible writers (John and Paul above all) tell us that this one truth *can be known* with God's grace and the Church's guidance.

John 8:31–32: Jesus then said to the Jews who had believed in him, "If you continue in my word, you are truly my disciples, and you will know the truth, and the truth will make you free" (cf. Luke 1:4; John 1:17; 4:23).

John 14:6: Jesus said to him, "I am the way, and the truth, and the life; no one comes to the Father, but by me."

John 16:13: "When the Spirit of truth comes, he will guide you into all the truth; for he will not speak on his own authority, but whatever he hears he will speak, and he will declare to you the things that are to come" (cf. 15:26; 18:37).

John 17:17, 19: "Sanctify them in the truth; thy word is truth. . . . And for their sake I consecrate myself, that they also may be consecrated in truth."

2 Corinthians 13:8: For we cannot do anything against the truth, but only for the truth (cf. 1 Cor. 2:13, Rom. 9:1).

Ephesians 6:14: Stand therefore, having girded your loins with truth, and having put on the breastplate of righteousness (cf. 1:13; Gal. 5:7; Phil. 4:8; Col. 1:3–10).

2 Timothy 1:14: Guard the truth that has been entrusted to you by the Holy Spirit who dwells within us (cf. 2:25; 1 Tim. 2:4; 4:3).

2 Timothy 3:7–8: Who will listen to anybody and can never arrive at a knowledge of the truth. As Jannes and Jambres

opposed Moses, so these men also oppose the truth, men of corrupt mind and counterfeit faith (cf. 4:4; Titus 1:1, 14; Heb. 10:26; James 5:19).

1 Peter 1:22: Having purified your souls by your obedience to the truth (cf. 2 Pet. 1:12).

1 John 2:21: I write to you, not because you do not know the truth, but because you know it, and know that no lie is of the truth (cf. 2:27; 3:19).

1 John 4:6: We are of God. Whoever knows God listens to us, and he who is not of God does not listen to us. By this we know the spirit of truth and the spirit of error (cf. 5:7; 2 John 1:1-2; 3 John 1:3-4, 12).

86. The Bible assumes one truth, not different levels of truth

Who decides what is essential doctrine and what is not? Where, moreover, is that differentiation found in Scripture? Where are we informed that certain truths are "non-essential" and therefore less important than others—to the point Christians need not even adhere to them?

Not in the Bible. In fact, the very notion of distinguishing between "essential" and "secondary" doctrines is unbiblical. Nowhere in Scripture do we find any implication that some things pertaining to doctrine and theology were optional, whereas others had to be believed. On the contrary, Jesus told us to "observe all that I have commanded you" (Matt. 28:19) without distinguishing between central and peripheral doctrines.

Likewise, Paul regards Christian Tradition as of one piece, not an amalgam of permissible competing theories: "the tradition that you received from us" (2 Thess. 3:6); "the truth which has been entrusted to you by the Holy Spirit" (2 Tim. 1:14); "the doctrine which you have been taught" (Rom. 16:17);

"stand firm in one spirit, with one mind striving side by side for the faith of the gospel," (Phil. 1:27).

He, like Jesus, ties doctrinal unity together with the one God: "Maintain the unity of the Spirit in the bond of peace. There is one body and one Spirit . . . one Lord, one faith, one baptism" (Eph. 4:3-5). Peter refers to one, unified "way of righteousness" and "the holy commandment delivered to them" (2 Pet. 2:21), while Jude urges us to "contend for the faith which was once for all delivered to the saints" (Jude 3). And Luke 2:42 casually mentions "the apostles' teaching" without any hint that there were competing interpretations of it, or variations of the teaching. Denominations, and all that they entail (particularly doctrinal contradiction or any sort of theological relativism), are clearly ruled out by Scripture—but they are inevitable products of *sola scriptura*.

It will do no good to say that unity in truth can't be achieved, or that it can be achieved only on (arbitrarily named) "central doctrines," because this idea is blatantly contrary to Scripture, which makes no such distinction (John 8:32; 14:6, 17; 14:26; 15:26; 16:13-15; 17:17-19; Rom. 1:18, 25; 1 Tim. 2:4; 3:15; 2 Tim. 3:7; 1 John 4:6; 5:6).

XII.
Counter-Arguments Against Alleged
Sola Scriptura Prooftexts

Before we proceed in this section, which addresses the most common alleged prooftexts to which Protestants appeal in their support for *sola scriptura*, the deficiencies of such prooftexting should be briefly explained. Bible verses that simply reiterate the trustworthiness and goodness of Scripture are not sufficient to prove *sola scriptura*. They *harmonize* with a *sola scriptura* outlook, but they do not *establish* it or provide any evidence in favor of it, for they are just as harmonious with the Catholic view.

With regard to a supposed biblical assertion of *sola scriptura*, no descriptive verse can be found—not even an indirect one— nor can a reasonable deduction for the same be drawn from what we see in Scripture. Such a hypothetical verse (if it in fact existed) would have to read something like this:

> Do not take heed of any written or oral traditions, as sufficient for the purposes of doctrine or action, since the written word of God in Holy Scripture is your ultimate and final authority, above any church or tradition.

Not only can no verse even remotely approaching this be found, many that directly contradict it *can* be: 1 Corinthians 11:2; 1 Thessalonians 2:13; 2 Thessalonians 2:15; 3:6, 1 Timothy 3:15; 2 Timothy 1:13-14; 2:2. Why would a statement such as the above hypothetical one *not* be in the Bible, if this principle is so supremely important?

Despite this, many Protestants contend that the Bible teaches the notion that it *alone* is infallibly authoritative, and they contend it in sometimes quite ingenious—though fallacious— ways. We shall, in closing, examine some of the more popular proposed Protestant prooftexts for *sola scriptura* and explain why they fail as logical or exegetical proof.

87. Deuteronomy 6:6-9: "These words which I command you"

> And these words which I command you this day shall be upon your heart; and you shall teach them diligently to your children, and shall talk of them when you sit in your house, and when you walk by the way, and when you lie down, and when you rise. And you shall bind them as a sign upon your hand, and they shall be as frontlets between your eyes. And you shall write them on the doorposts of your house and on your gates.

The Jews were urged to teach the Law to their children, but that doesn't prove, or even imply, *sola scriptura* (as the Protestant contention would have it), because this command doesn't exist in isolation from other passages that indicate a system of authority and authoritative interpretation. Deuteronomy 6:6-9 is an exhortation for parents to be responsible in the religious upbringing of their children, not an obtuse clue that someday written Scripture would be the sole rule of faith.

88. Psalms 119:159-160: "Thy word is truth"

> Consider how I love thy precepts! Preserve my life according to thy steadfast love. The sum of thy word is truth; and every one of thy righteous ordinances endures forever.

Again, we see an exercise common in such alleged "evidence": assuming what one is trying to prove, sometimes called circular reasoning or "begging the question." This passage simply doesn't *rule out* other authorities. No Christian would argue against what the text says: God's word is truth. Of course it is! But this is no proof of the Protestant novelty that is *sola scriptura*. The notion supposedly being supported isn't even present in the text. It is merely read into it, or superimposed onto it. Protestants think *sola scriptura* is "obvious" and "unquestionable" in the way that a fish in an aquarium thinks it is "obvious" that the entire world consists of water and that all creatures live in it.

If *sola scriptura* is all one knows or hears about, then of course one will come away with that viewpoint. But remove the Protestant's set of presumptions (which must be argued for, not used as evidence), and the plain meaning of this passage does nothing to support *sola scriptura*.

89. Proverbs 30:5-6: "Every word of God proves true"

Every word of God proves true; he is a shield to those who take refuge in him. Do not add to his words, lest he rebuke you, and you be found a liar.

The Protestant who utilizes this passage as a prooftext is assuming that support for, extolling, praising, and lifting up the Bible as a standard equates to support of the Bible as the only infallible rule of faith. This is not the case: They're two different things. The inspired revelation is pure and uncontaminated (no one disagrees), but this doesn't logically (or biblically) rule out *other* sources of truth; otherwise, Jesus and the apostles would not have cited other sources in order to back up their claims.

90. Isaiah 40:8: God's word "will stand forever"

The grass withers, the flower fades; but the word of our God will stand forever.

If God's word stands forever, then it must be the sole infallible standard of faith: that is the Protestant argument, which is no more than an assumed premise, utterly inadequate to establish *sola scriptura*. Indeed, the word of God does stand forever, but this passage does not say that it stands *alone*, in alleged contrast to Church and apostolic Tradition. That is the hidden assumption that causes Protestants to think such verses are compelling evidence for *sola scriptura*.

I could state, "The Washington Monument stands forever." Would that mean that there are no *other* monuments or edifices? I could say, "The Constitution stands forever." Would that mean that there could be no Congress to write new laws in accordance with it, or a president to enact them, or a Supreme Court to interpret whether such laws are harmonious with the Constitution? By analogy, we see how weak these "arguments" really are.

91. Matthew 24:35: "My words will not pass away"

"Heaven and earth will pass away, but my words will not pass away."

The Protestant argues that this expression of the permanency of Jesus' words—the words of the Word of God—makes Scripture unique. We readily agree that Scripture is unique. But neither uniqueness nor inspiration make something the sole rule of faith.

This passage is further insufficient as a proof of *sola scriptura* because, according to Scripture (and, I would say, common sense), Jesus' words are not *confined* to Scripture. Jesus was not a "talking Bible machine" (see John 20:30; 21:25; Acts 1:2-3).

This argument presupposes that Jesus was always talking only about his words that were recorded in Scripture, and thus begs the question. It also has no scriptural warrant: In Matthew 28:19-20, in the "Great Commission" passage, Jesus tells the disciples to evangelize and baptize, "teaching them to observe all that I have commanded you" (28:20).

There is no reason (textually or contextually) to believe that he intended the "all" here to be confined to what eventually was recorded in the Gospels. Since there was no written New

Testament at that time, the disciples who heard Jesus say this would have understood the Lord as telling them to pass on to others what they had learned *orally* from him. Moreover, we have no record of Jesus himself writing anything that has been passed down to us.

92. John 20:30-31: "These are written that you may believe"

Now Jesus did many other signs in the presence of the disciples, which are not written in this book; but these are written that you may believe that Jesus is the Christ, the Son of God, and that believing you may have life in his name.

The Bible communicates the gospel that saves. This doesn't prove the principle of *sola scriptura*. It doesn't exclude the Church or Tradition (or any Catholic distinctive). In fact, in verse 20:30 John refers to things Jesus did (which would surely include teaching) that he did *not* record in his Gospel. Thus, a meaning of "written only" (let alone the involved theory of *sola scriptura*) is precluded even in the immediate context.

93. Acts 15:15: "The words of the prophets agree"

And with this the words of the prophets agree, as it is written...

Protestants argue in this instance that, since the Jerusalem Council appealed to the words of the prophets, recorded in Scripture, then Scripture *alone* is normative for determination of doctrine. This is viewed as an explicit example of the methodology of *sola scriptura*.

James, the bishop of Jerusalem, utilized Scripture (we know from the biblical account), but there's a fallacy in thinking that this form of "argument from authority" is all-inclusive. An appeal to Scripture doesn't rule out appeal to other infallible authorities. We know that in the New Testament itself, for instance, sources not in the Old Testament were cited as authoritative (as we saw in No. 13 above). The deuterocanonical books rejected by Protestants are also utilized in the New Testament (see No. 16), and oral tradition is deemed to be authoritative as well as written Scripture (Nos. 20-21). Therefore, Acts 15:15 alone is by no means a prooftext for *sola scriptura*.

Moreover, the quotation of the Old Testament in Acts 15:16-18 does not directly address the main controversy at hand: whether male Gentiles needed to be circumcised (15:1-2). It was merely a general treatment that Gentiles were eventually to be included in God's covenant and salvation. In the record we have of this council, no mention is made of any Old Testament texts about circumcision.

We may reasonably assume that some were discussed, but nevertheless, based on what we *know*, no one can definitively conclude that such passages were the "clincher" for the argument that Gentiles need not continue the practice. The final decision is not expressed in terms of some semblance of *sola scriptura*, but rather as an example of Church authority, led by God: "For it has seemed good to the Holy Spirit and to us to lay upon you no greater burden" (Acts 15:28).

By now we see the strong pattern of these alleged prooftexts for *sola scriptura*: simplistic exegesis of Scripture, and reading into passages (*eisegesis*) things that go beyond what is actually present. Most of those who use these "proofs" regard them as virtually self-evident and in need of no further explication.

Vigorously asserting a fallacy doesn't make it *not* a fallacy. Unproven things don't become true by virtue of mere repetition. Truth in theology is not arrived at through the propaganda technique of stating things again and again so that people accept them without thinking them through.

Catholics appeal to Scripture just as much as Protestants do in matters of doctrine, morals, and worship. But Catholics know that appeals to Scripture must be guided by an *interpreting authority*. After all, in this very citation, in the context of the council at

Jerusalem, James, the bishop of Jerusalem, reaches an authoritative decision based on the statement of Peter, who had previously spoken definitively (15:7-11). The council is entirely in line with Catholic thought, even down to a "papal pronouncement"!

Furthermore, the book of Acts (the larger context) condemns the sectarianism and division so typical of Protestantism (4:32), and refers explicitly to bishops (20:28; cf. 20:17). It is in Acts as well (1:20-26) that we find an explicit biblical proof of apostolic succession, a key element of the Catholic ecclesiological viewpoint, over against the Protestant notion of *sola scriptura*.

94. Galatians 1:8-9: "A gospel contrary to that which you received"

> But even if we, or an angel from heaven, should preach to you a gospel contrary to that which we preached to you, let him be accursed. As we have said before, so now I say again, if anyone is preaching to you a gospel contrary to that which you received, let him be accursed.

In appealing to this verse, Protestants assume that the gospel received was in written form only; therefore, *sola scriptura* is normative. Anything that goes beyond this gospel and which cannot be explicitly grounded in Scripture (including most of Catholic Tradition) is to be "accursed." It is essentially an "anti-traditional" rather than pro-*sola scriptura* argument. A more sophisticated version would contend that the gospel was originally preached, but later inscripturated in Paul's letters, and that this would preclude Catholic traditions that are not explicitly (or, they say, implicitly) taught in the Bible.

But Paul doesn't confine his apostolic gospel message to the words of Scripture. For him there is also oral proclamation, described as tradition. Here he is distinguishing between true Christian Tradition and false (heresy), not between written authority and oral—let alone between the Church and the Bible.

Those are simply unsubstantiated opinions that a Protestant brings to the text (eisegesis), not points expressed in the text itself (another example of circular *sola scriptura* reasoning).

Nothing here would establish the notion of "Scripture as the only infallible authority." In fact, Paul is not even referring to his writing but to his "preaching." How, then, can this be said to refer to Scripture? In fact, this terminology of "preached" or "delivered" and hearers or readers "receiving" the Christian message is used by Paul of *tradition* (1 Cor. 11:2; 2 Thess. 2:15; 3:6) and *word of God* (1 Thess. 2:13) in the same way as he uses it in relation to the gospel (1 Cor. 15:1; Gal. 1:9; 1 Thess. 2:9).

For Paul, the three descriptions are synonymous. Therefore, no one can drive a wedge between Tradition and the gospel or the written Bible, and this passage fails as a prooftext for *sola scriptura*.

95. 2 Timothy 3:15-17: "All scripture is inspired by God"

> But as for you, continue in what you have learned and have firmly believed, knowing from whom you learned it and how from childhood you have been acquainted with the sacred writings which are able to instruct you for salvation through faith in Christ Jesus. All scripture is inspired by God and profitable for teaching, for reproof, for correction, and for training in righteousness, that the man of God may be complete, equipped for every good work.

This is the classic Protestant prooftext for *sola scriptura*. The hidden premise is that, since Scripture is good for all *these* things, it is good for *all* things, including being the sole infallible rule of faith.

But the second doesn't follow from the first. Catholics who understand their faith abide by this passage as much as Protestants do. But a plain reading shows that "equipping for every good work" does not exclude other sources of training, as *sola scriptura* would demand.

If the apostle Paul were, in fact, teaching *sola scriptura* here, then he certainly contradicts himself in many other places in his biblical writings. The important notions of Church and Tradition are present implicitly in 2 Timothy 3:15-16, based on topically cross-referencing to other Pauline passages on authority, apostolic Tradition, and the Church. Moreover, if we look at the overall context of this passage, in 2 Timothy alone Paul makes reference to oral tradition three times (1:13-14; 2:2; 3:14).

In 2 Thessalonians 2:15, Paul instructs his readers to follow his instruction whether by *letter* or *word of mouth* (many other such indications of the authority of tradition have been examined elsewhere in this book). Some Protestants counter argue that Paul is merely giving a pastoral injunction to the Thessalonians and is not laying down a binding principle about the unquestionable authority of oral tradition. But by the same token, we could just as well say that 2 Timothy 3:15-16 falls in the same category and was not intended as an eternal decree about the authority of *sola scriptura*, over against Church and Tradition. The oral tradition was just as binding in Paul's opinion as his written letters.

We agree with Protestants that Scripture can train us in righteousness and equip us for good works, just as we believe in the material sufficiency of the Bible (the notion that all Christian doctrines are found in Scripture in some form or other). The Protestant mistake lies in equating that sufficiency with *formal* sufficiency: the Bible as the sole, ultimate, binding norm and authoritative rule of faith, to the exclusion of Church and Tradition.

This doesn't follow logically or exegetically from the passage. It is a circular argument. At best, this passage might be regarded as *harmonious* with a view of *sola scriptura*, assuming it were clearly established on other biblical grounds. But in no way does it *establish* the principle of *sola scriptura*.

96. James 1:18: "The word of truth"

> Of his own will he brought us forth by the word of truth that we should be a kind of first fruits of his creatures.

Any biblical concordance will reveal that "word" (*logos*) in Scripture by no means refers to written words only (let alone just the Bible). Paul, in fact, does not equate but contrasts *logos* with the written word in, for example, 2 Thessalonians 2:15, where he effectively equates *logos* with oral tradition or proclamation. "Word" in Scripture is used far more to refer to preaching than to a collection of writings. Yet, many Protestants, and specifically defenders of *sola scriptura*, see "word" and they immediately equate it with Scripture. This is a serious exegetical error.

97. 1 Peter 1:23: "The living and abiding word of God"

> You have been born anew, not of perishable seed but of imperishable, through the living and abiding word of God.

Sola scriptura Protestants believe that "word of God" here refers to the Bible, which (it would follow according to this verse) is essential not only to doctrine but also to salvation itself. Therefore, it alone can be the infallible standard. Romans 10:17 is utilized similarly. In the King James Version it reads: "So then faith cometh by hearing and hearing by the word of God."

Again, it is casually assumed that written Scripture is being referenced. But this is such a questionable conclusion that the Revised Standard Version renders the same verse, "So faith comes from what is heard, and what is heard comes by the *preaching of Christ*" (italics mine).

As usual, then, Protestants using this passage as a supposed proof of *sola scriptura* are engaging in circular reasoning (assuming what they're trying to prove). Peter defines "word" in context (1:25) as "the good news that was announced to you." He is referring to the gospel itself—the gospel that was preached, and was not synonymous with "the Bible," as the New Testament did not yet exist. It is another instance of casually assuming that "word" is referring to the Bible alone, even though that's not how it is usually used in the New (or Old) Testament.

98. 2 Peter 3:15-16: Paul's letters described by Peter as Scripture

> And count the forbearance of our Lord as salvation. So also our beloved brother Paul wrote to you according to the wisdom given him, speaking of this as he does in all his letters. There are some things in them hard to understand, which the ignorant and unstable twist to their own destruction, as they do the other scriptures.

Catholics wholeheartedly agree that this passage shows there is such a thing as written revelation, and that it is supremely important in the Christian life. But this is irrelevant to the question of whether *sola scriptura* is true and biblical.

One cannot prove *sola scriptura* simply by citing passages about the value of written scriptures. That the Bible affirms that a written Scripture exists and possesses inspiration and authority does not prove that it is formally sufficient (the sole and final rule of faith, over and against Church or Tradition). Protestants need to show that that the Bible affirms Scripture as the sole rule of faith, excluding the authority of Church and Tradition. This passage does not do this, as indeed *no* Bible passage does.

99. 1 John 2:27: "No need that anyone should teach you"

> But the anointing which you received from him abides in you, and you have no need that anyone should teach you; as his anointing teaches you about everything, and is true, and is no lie, just as it has taught you, abide in him.

Protestants of a certain sort, who frown upon denominational affiliations, creeds, and formal Christian doctrine, often produce this passage. They argue, based on this verse, that teachers are unnecessary (an assumption quite congenial to more extreme factions of the *sola scriptura* outlook) because it is interpreted in a literal way.

But in this verse we find typical Hebraic hyperbole, clearly not meant to be taken literally: similar to "Call no man your father on earth" (Matt. 23:9) or, "If anyone comes to me and does not hate his own father and mother and wife and children" (Luke 14:26). The same author calls himself an "elder" (2 John and 3 John 1:1), so obviously *he is himself teaching* in these three letters; therefore, a literal interpretation (that since we have the Bible, no one needs a teacher) is impossible.

The Bible specifically mentions authoritative "teaching." Acts 2:41–42 refers to "apostles' teaching"; Paul mentions "the standard of teaching" (Rom. 6:17) and "the teaching" (1 Tim. 6:1); thus illustrating that there is no such concept in the New Testament of a "Lone Ranger" Christian, accountable to no one and nothing but the Bible.

100. Revelation 22:18–19: Adding words to the book is forbidden

> I warn everyone who hears the words of the prophecy of this book: if any one adds to them, God will add to him the plagues described in this book, and if any one takes away from the words of the book of this prophecy, God will take away his share in the tree of life and in the holy city, which are described in this book.

This refers only to the book of Revelation (as seen in the words "if any man shall take away from the words of the book of this prophecy"). Not all Scripture is prophetic in nature. That is all it is referring to. It does not in any way prohibit an authoritative extra-scriptural or oral teaching.

Of course no one can or should "add" words to a biblical book. It is inspired, and is what it is. As with the others we've examined, however, this prooftext is used by people who seem to forget just what it is they are trying to prove: *sola scriptura,* the idea that the Bible is the only infallible authority and rule of faith. It fails because one book of the Bible is not the whole

Bible, and also because this has to do with the canon (or limits) of Scripture, rather than its function or relation to the Church and to apostolic Tradition.

It is also illogical to conclude (as some Protestant apologists do) that because no one can add words to inspired Scripture (a notion with which Catholics agree but deny is taught in Revelation 22:18-19, for the reasons above), therefore all authority besides written Scripture is non-infallible or inherently objectionable. It is (again) the smuggled assumption that doesn't follow, since the Bible sanctions authoritative Tradition and an infallible Church.

Conclusion

One who truly follows Scripture wherever it leads, and who isn't beholden to a tradition of men invented in the sixteenth century, will conclude that *sola scriptura* is unbiblical, illogical, and untrue. I submit that the foregoing demonstrates its biblical and intellectual bankruptcy from many angles.

To briefly summarize the extended critique in these pages: First, we have seen how an authoritative, binding Tradition—a notion contradictory to *sola scriptura*—is repeatedly assumed in the Bible. This holds true even for oral tradition and deuterocanonical tradition (the so-called "apocryphal" books that Protestants don't accept; therefore, for them, they are "extrabiblical").

We've also learned from Scripture that our Lord Jesus and the apostles accepted the legitimacy of Jewish tradition, and the authority structure of pre-Christian Judaism. For them, the system of the Old Covenant was not completed by the New, but rather was built upon and developed into Christianity. All of that is inconsistent with *sola scriptura* as well—as explained.

We've observed how "word of the Lord" and "word of God" usually, in Scripture, refer to oral proclamation, not the written word, let alone the Bible. We noted the many difficulties of Scripture's "perspicuity" and of authoritative interpretation. We have discovered from the Bible that the Church is authoritative and has binding, infallible authority, ordained by God. This, too, runs contrary to *sola scriptura*. The Bible teaches one thing; the man-made tradition of *sola scriptura* says another.

We have unpacked the implications of apostolic succession, the Jerusalem Council, and many analogies to infallible Church authority. We have exposed the severely flawed nature of denominationalism and doctrinal indifferentism and supposed uncertainty of so-called "secondary doctrines." Lastly, we have observed how the classic alleged prooftexts for *sola scriptura* fail to prove this principle from the Bible.

It is a good policy to pursue and follow biblical truth. The inspired, inerrant Bible (God's written revelation to man) teaches about authority, presenting a three-legged stool of Bible-Church-Tradition. It does *not* teach *sola scriptura*. How much proof is needed for a person to accept that manifest fact? This book is intended as a tool to help seekers analyze the biblical data that can be brought to bear, in order to arrive at an informed, biblical conclusion.

Persuading Protestants to *analyze the issue at all*, and to dare to question the veracity of one of their foundational premises, is more than half the battle. Even if I can achieve only that much, I shall feel that this effort has been successful. But of course I hope that I can persuade readers that the idea is false and unworthy of belief, because the Bible teaches contrary truths.

Endnotes

1   *Dogmatic Canons and Decrees of the Council of Trent, Vatican Council I, Plus the Decree on the Immaculate Conception and the Syllabus of Errors of Pope Pius IX* (New York: Devin-Adair Company, 1912; reprinted: Rockford, Illinois: TAN Books and Publishers, Inc., 1977); Session III, document dated 24 April 1870; this portion from p. 221.

2   Norman L. Geisler and Ralph E. Mackenzie, *Roman Catholics and Evangelicals: Agreements and Differences* (Grand Rapids, Michigan: Baker Books, 1995), p. 178.

3   Mathison, Keith A., *The Shape of Sola Scriptura* (Moscow, Idaho: Canon Press, 2001), pp. 259-260.

4   *Ibid.*, p. 269.

5   White, James R., *The Roman Catholic Controversy* (Minneapolis: Bethany House Publishers, 1996), pp. 56-62; all italics in the original; some ellipses indicating text in between the bullet points are eliminated for the sake of presentation.

6   Midrash Rabbah Vayikra 1:2

7   "Jimmy Akin More Than a Decade Behind," 6-8-06, http://www.aomin.org/aoblog/index.php?itemid=1393

8   Whitaker, William, *A disputation on Holy Scripture, against the papists, especially Bellarmine and Stapleton*, from the online version, translated and edited by William Fitzgerald and published by The University Press, Cambridge, in 1849: http://www.archive.org/stream/disputationonhol00whituoft/disputationonhol00whituoft_djvu.txt

9   Exodus Rabbah 43:4 and the Pesiktade-RavKahana 1:7

10 available online (public domain): http://www.jewishencyclopedia.com/articles/12358-priest

11 *The Roman Catholic Controversy* (Minneapolis: Bethany House Publishers, 1996), 97-98.

12 *Answers to Catholic Claims* (Southbridge, Massachusetts: Crowne Publications, Inc., 1990), p. 56; italics his own.

13 Whitaker, William, *A disputation on Holy Scripture, against the papists, especially Bellarmine and Stapleton*, from the online version, translated and edited by William Fitzgerald and published by the University

Press, Cambridge, in 1849: http://www.archive.org/stream/disputa-
tiononhol00whituoft/disputationonhol00whituoft_djvu.txt, p. 652.

14 *The Roman Catholic Controversy* (Minneapolis: Bethany House Publishers, 1996), p. 59; italics his own.

15 In his *Fundamentals of Catholic Dogma* (edited in English by James
Canon Bastible; translated by Patrick Lynch; Rockford, Illinois: TAN
Books and Publishers, Inc., fourth edition, 1960; reprinted 1974), pp.
296-298, Ludwig Ott argues from the indwelling of the Holy Spirit
and presence of Christ to the indefectibility of the Church, saying,
"The intrinsic reason for the indefectibility of the Church of Christ
lies in her inner relation with Christ, who is the Foundation of the
Church (I Cor. 3,11) and with the Holy Ghost, who indwells in her as
essence and life-principle." He cites St. Irenaeus, St. Augustine, and
St. Thomas Aquinas along the same lines. The Catechism makes the
same argument, though not as explicitly linked with indefectibility,
in 797-798.